TRACY COLLINS BANK

TRACY
COLLINS
BANK &
TRUST
COMPANY

# TRACY COLLINS BANK & TRUST COMPANY

*A Record of Responsibility 1884-1984*

Leonard J. Arrington

EDEN HILL
Midvale, Utah

ISBN 0-941214-25-7
Printed in the United States of America
Eden Hill Publishing, Midvale, Utah

# Contents

# Preface

One hundred years ago, Chester A. Arthur was serving as President of the United States, Victoria was celebrating her forty-seventh year as Queen of the United Kingdom of Great Britain and Ireland and Empress of India, and the first long-distance telephone line was constructed by Bell Telephone. New inventions being introduced in 1884 included calculating machines, telephones, dynamos, electric lighting, Kodak cameras, safety razors, electric irons, linotype machines, and the first prototype automobiles. It was a fruitful year. James Whitcomb Riley's *The Old Swimmin'-Hole,* Mark Twain's *Adventures of Huckleberry Finn,* and Robert Louis Stevenson's *Treasure Island* had just come out, and the Metropolitan Opera House had just been opened. In the West, the mood was expansive—and not always in a properly organized fashion. In 1884, "boomers" settled on two million acres of Oklahoma in a scene that resembled bedlam. Simultaneously, farm prices declined, a reversal of years of agricultural prosperity that would ruin many farmers and small towns.

That was the year Russel Lord Tracy, not yet twenty-five, established a small banking business in Cheyenne, Wyoming, which, since its reestablishment in Salt Lake City in 1892, has grown into a $300 million enterprise, with eighteen branches or banking outlets in this regional capital.

This centennial of Tracy-Collins Bank and Trust Company is an occasion for remembrance. We remember

Russel Lord Tracy, the young Ohio consumptive who came west for his health and founded an enterprise which, because of his careful management, exceeded all expectations. We remember James W. Collins, the Salt Lake City newspaper boy, who was an officer of Tracy-Collins Bank and Trust Company and its predecessors for almost half a century; Newell B. Dayton, an energetic and popular executive for a similar long period; and Gil Shelton, "the boy from Missouri," who was president and chairman of the board from 1970 to 1982. Finally, we remember the "aggressive but safe" leadership of John A. Dahlstrom who, with others, purchased Tracy-Collins Bank and Trust Company in 1969, and, with the help of Charles R. Canfield who joined the company in 1970, strengthened its market position, doubled its assets, and made the enterprise one of the top seven banks in Utah.

In writing the history I am particularly grateful to both "oldtimers" and the current management—to Russel Lord Tracy, who left extensive memoirs; to James W. Collins, whose record of service has been clearly organized and easy to follow; to Newell Dayton, Gil Shelton, and Blaine Simons, who have helped me recapture much of the history; and to many officers and employees of Tracy-Collins who have been unfailingly courteous and generous.

John Alley, Jr., a brilliant and versatile young historian from the University of Utah and the University of California at Santa Barbara, was an industrious, efficient, and talented research assistant, and his work was so perceptive and extensive as to be tantamount to collaboration. Christine Waters did stenographic work and typing, and Scott Kenney and Mary Ann Flandro of Eden Hill Publishing were always helpful and prompt.

Above all, I am grateful to Ronald J. Swenson,

former senior vice president, to Charles R. Canfield, president, and to John A. Dahlstrom, chairman of the board, for their expert assistance and constant encouragement to write this history according to the highest professional standards.

22 June 1984 Leonard J. Arrington

CHAPTER *1*

# Russel Lord Tracy: Taking Root in Cheyenne

In 1877, during their flight across the West, the Nez Perce Indians had passed through Yellowstone National Park and met tourist parties along the way, encounters which aptly symbolized the changing character and human significance of the western wilderness. The geologic fantasy had, in 1872, become the first national park in the United States. Although the days of massive tourism were still a few years down the road, Yellowstone rapidly became a popular spot for those who were willing to endure minor privation in the cause of outdoor recreation. One expedition that arrived to rough it in luxury entered the park in August 1883. The President of the United States Chester A. Arthur, had come West to view the park's boiling, bubbling wonders, accompanied by Secretary of War Robert T. Lincoln, Senator George G. Vest of Missouri, Montana Governor John S. Crosby, Lieutenant General Philip H. Sheridan, then making his third visit to the park, and assorted other dignitaries. They drove over the still primitive roads in three spring wagons escorted by a troop of the Fifth United States Cavalry with 150 pack mules trailing behind. They carried among other things china, crystal, sterling silver, and linen.[1] The twenty-three-year-old Ohioan who had been responsible for selecting their outfit recalled that

> . . . in order to provide a dinner and breakfast for them the chef was engaged from the Palace Hotel in San Francisco. Each guest had a new wall tent with a wagon cover for a carpet and each tent contained comfortable new beds, blankets, etc. The dining room consisted of a new hospital tent which contained a mahogany table and chairs shipped from Major Lord's private home with fine linen, glasses, and silverware, all in charge of his private butler who accompanied them. We also took from his home a fifteen-lamp chandelier so that upon the arrival in camp they enjoyed all the comforts and luxuries which they could find either in Washington or San Francisco.[2]

This hospitable Major James H. Lord was the uncle of the young camp sutler, Russel Lord Tracy, who, the next year, came West again to renew his own love affair with Yellowstone and conduct some important business with his father and three other gentlemen from Ohio. This perhaps was not the most obvious setting for the founding of a financial enterprise which would grow to become Tracy-Collins Bank & Trust, one of the largest banks in the Mountain West. But for Tracy, a man who loved the outdoors and Yellowstone in particular, it was an appropriate locale. He had first come to the park in 1881 as a member of an expedition led by General Sheridan. This and Sheridan's second trip, persuaded the general, an enormously popular Civil War hero, to rally public concern over the administration of the park and public support for increased appropriations to improve and protect it. For twenty-one-year-old Tracy, who had just taken up residence in Cheyenne because of weak lungs, it offered a chance to visit battle grounds where General Oliver Otis Howard's troops had squared off with Chief Joseph's Nez Perces, to hear tales of the fighting from Howard's soldiers; to see the site of the much earlier Fetterman fight with the Sioux at Old Fort Phil Kearny (Wyoming, 1866); to delight in Mammoth Hot Springs which "contained millions of little coral cups from the size of a thimble to several feet in diameter, all filled and running over with hot boiling water containing a strong solution of lime"; to catch a two-pound trout in Yellowstone Lake and then "by a simple twist of the wrist" cook it in a nearby boiling hot spring; and to wonder at Old Faithful, Excelsior, the Castle, the Giant, the Riverside, and other geysers.[3]

Tracy's return in 1884 with his father and the other Ohioans was only one of many regular pilgrimages. But that year as they left the park via the Snake River on the west, near the site of the Tracy Club he would eventually found for his employees, Tracy listened to his companions' advice and decided to enter the mortgage loan business, with the three of them as his first investors. This decision not only launched him on an emphatically successful career but also gave him a permanent role in a growing region, a role which drew strength from its connection with his former home in Ohio.

Russel Tracy, at the age of twenty-one, had already had an active life.[4] He was born on September 15, 1860, to Fred Earl Tracy and Anna Lord Tracy of Mansfield, Ohio, the third of their five children. A prosperous Mansfield grocer, his father was also a devout Congregationalist and an active philanthropist, traits that he passed on to his son. In the elder Tracy's business, accounts were always kept carefully balanced except for the often-red benevolent account. Mr. Tracy explained that "I have frequently found that when without funds in this account if I contributed to some worthy charity out of other accounts the Lord always assisted me in securing the money and putting the account in the black again." Young Russel especially remembered his father's habit of fattening several dozen turkeys each year, destined to become the Thanksgiving dinners of widows and poor families. Years later in Salt Lake City Russel Tracy was well known for his custom of providing newsboys with Thanksgiving dinners.

Anna Lord came from a substantial family which included a step-aunt and sister who were President Benjamin Harrison's first and second wives. Her father, Russel F. Lord, was Chief Engineer and General Superintendent of the Delaware and Hudson Canal Company. Anna's brother, James H. Lord, pursued a successful military career and, as quartermaster at Cheyenne, introduced Russel to the West.

Russel Tracy's childhood memories reflect a wholesome and free-spirited Midwestern upbringing suitable to an upper middle class youth. He delighted in hunting squirrels or occasionally some unsuspecting farmer's chickens, or raising his own chickens. He received his own much-desired Christmas rooster after scheming to give one to his younger sister because he knew, like any child, that she must want one as much as he. At sixteen he was off to Oberlin College, a bastion of the old frontier's reform and evangelistic traditions which in 1837 had become the first college to permit women to enroll. His sister Lou was already there. The innovation of coeducation did not imply a liberal attitude in other areas. Only ten years before Russel's arrival, Charles Grandison

Finney, the best known evangelist of his era, had ended a fifteen-year presidency of the school. Oberlin's strict code prohibited tobacco, card games, dances, and the theater. Male students were not permitted to "take girls out buggy riding and were expected to be in [their] rooms by ten o'clock at night." However, Tracy's independent streak led him to the secret room over a drug store which some "more venturesome" students had rented to play cards and smoke cigarettes. Dances at nearby Elyria provided an alternative to the staid academic halls. When an informer brought suspensions to some of these freer-spirits, he was tarred and feathered, an action which led to more suspensions, threatened legal prosecution, and a near riot of the studentbody.[5]

Russel had to leave this adventurous college career behind before he could graduate, for a recurring consumptive condition became life-threatening. On doctor's orders he traveled to Minnesota under care of his older sister in the summer of 1877. Tuberculosis would soon decline from its long-standing position as one of the most common infectious diseases of the Western world when Robert Koch, five years later, in 1882, discovered the causative bacillus, and efforts to control its propagation would rapidly increase.[6] It would, however, plague Russel Tracy for several years and become a major reason for his travels in the West. After a summer spent traveling by horse and buggy around Minnesota Russel's health had improved enough for Lou to leave him at a lumber camp. Here he developed a fondness for a burly lumberjack named Big Mike who turned out to be wanted for murder committed in a barroom brawl. When the law caught up to Mike, Russel was as surprised as anyone but took pains to reassure his parents that the values of right and wrong they had instilled in him were still intact.

Youthful ignorance soon brought Tracy into another unintended encounter with the law. But at least this time he obtained his first experience as an independent businessman in the process:

> By spring [of 1878] I had greatly improved in health, but realized that I must spend as much time as possible out-of-doors. I then wrote to my father, who was supporting my brother and three sisters at college and had his hands full, that if he would advance me enough to buy a gross of buggy whips, I could sell them at a profit, be out-of-doors all the time, see the country, pay my own expenses, and gain a little business experience.
>
> From the first I found this business very satisfactory, especially in the country. I could sell each whip at a profit of 100 to 150 per cent and yet sell cheaper than the stores.
>
> Later I became ambitious and entered the larger cities where the merchants would not permit street peddlers, without licenses. However, in St. Paul I found it profitable to work in the suburbs and catch the farmers as they drove into or out of the city. Even then I was taught that "all good things come to an end." One morning a big, uniformed, helmeted policeman arrested me for selling whips without a license and started to take me to the police station. After walking a few blocks in the sun he decided to let me go, but told me where to buy my license. When I learned the license would cost $50 I was discouraged and went home to my boarding house. After a refreshing sleep my courage revived and I decided to try the other side of town, where I would escape this particular policeman.
>
> I was soon singing my song and demonstrating my whips to the farmers when I saw, evidently on his way home from his beat, this same six-foot-plus policeman. I cut short my story to the farmers, gathered up my whips, hurried to the nearest alley where I broke into a run, hoping to get through before he could follow and see me turn right or left. But the boys in the neighborhood with all their dogs started in hot pursuit and I was overtaken.

This time, neither the sun nor my arguments proved of any avail, and I was kept in custody until brought before the judge. The policeman made a very bitter attack upon me, grossly exaggerating my offense, and claiming that I, like most street peddlers, was a menace to society. The result was that the judge imposed a fine of $50 or five days in jail.

This aroused me to the seriousness of my position and I asked if I could not be represented by a lawyer and the judge replied, "I see no reason why you should have an attorney since you admit your guilt, hence it is my duty to sentence you."

But I said, "I am guilty of selling whips without a license and may be called a peddler, but am not such a one as he described; further, because one peddler pretending to sell a kitchen knife used that as an excuse to enter many homes and rob them of everything movable, or because another peddler selling rugs became acquainted with the house and learned where the woman kept her money and later returned to rob and in a scuffle with her husband killed him, is no reason I should be classed with them and pronounced dangerous and a menace to society and punished accordingly."

I told him that I did not have $50 or any friends nearer than my home in Mansfield, Ohio; that it would be an awful disgrace to me and my family to be sent to jail and thereafter be known as a "jailbird." I also told him that I had been taught the difference between right and wrong according to God's laws, but I knew little of man-made laws, that I thought I had been doing good rather than harm, in that by sending money to Connecticut for my whips I was rewarding the man who made them, and by selling them to the farmer at a saving of from 50 cents to 75 cents on the whip, he would have that much more money to spend for clothes and food for his family, and that the profit I made would assist me in continuing my education. Further, I was a boy only eighteen, not strong enough to do heavy work, and that the doctor had ordered me to spend all my time out-of-doors. Even now, though

> convicted, I could not see that I had committed any sin or should be punished by being sent to jail.
>
> After further deliberation the sentence was suspended, provided I promised not to sell any more whips in St. Paul and to leave town in twenty-four hours. This I was glad to do.[7]

Following this brief encounter with nineteenth-century business regulation, Tracy returned to school, studying at Carleton College in Northfield, Minnesota. Within a couple of years, though, his health had deteriorated so drastically that his doctor told him that he probably had only a short time to live and recommended, as the best medicine, doing that of which he had always dreamed. Tracy had such a dream. He would sail to China from San Francisco using the inheritance of $2,000 his grandfather had left him, due on his twenty-first birthday.[8] He set off in the fall of 1881.

One apparently unanticipated part of the rail journey was crossing the Rocky Mountains. Sherman's Pass, the highest point on the Union Pacific line, was a reputed death trip for consumptives and the conductor on Tracy's train refused to carry him past Cheyenne. Tracy, undeniably ill, was carried by stretcher to a local hotel. Upon telegraphing his parents, he learned that by convenient coincidence his uncle, Captain and Brevet Major James H. Lord, had recently been appointed United States Army Quartermaster at Cheyenne Depot. Through this serendipity, Russel Tracy came to reside in Cheyenne, Wyoming, a town and region living on credit and ripe with opportunity for those, like Tracy, who would help provide some of that credit.

Cheyenne was a "hell-on-wheels" town, one of the raucous, transitory villages of construction workers and camp followers built in 1867 along the Union Pacific

Railroad. It managed to outlast those events, however, because of its strategic location at the eastern base of the Rocky Mountains where it provided access to the transcontinental railroad for a vast segment of the western interior. It grew so fast it earned the nickname, "Magic City of the Plains." During the 1870s Cheyenne also earned a reputation as the archetypal violent and freewheeling cowtown.[9] It may have had a wild and lively reputation, but a visitor in 1877 recorded a different impression: "Of all the forlorn, homesick looking towns, Cheyenne never had an equal.... Without a spear of grass, without a tree within scope of the eye, without water except as it was pumped up for domestic use, with a soil sandy, hard and barren—that was the raw Cheyenne in the '70s."[10]

Tracy arrived in 1880 just as Cheyenne was entering six years of the biggest boom the western cattle industry had ever seen. In 1880 Wyoming Territory had a population of only 20,789 people—up from the 9,118 of 1870. Laramie County was home for 6,400—5,047 of them in Cheyenne itself. Most ranch owners who could afford it preferred the social life of Cheyenne to the lonely plains, and cattle barons had already begun to erect ostentatious mansions along Carey Avenue, so they built homes in town and visited their ranches in season. The famous Cheyenne Club, heart and soul of the High Plains beef industry, was built in 1880. In 1883 Cheyenne installed what is said to have been the first electric lighting system in any city in the United States. Most important, investment funds from the East and overseas were flowing into the region, magnetized by the enormous profits possible in cattle and land.

Part of the staying power of Cheyenne during the 1870s had been provided by its military installations, Fort

D. A. Russell and Cheyenne Depot, popularly known as Camp Carlin. Major Lord arrived at Camp Carlin to take over as depot Quartermaster on June 30, 1880. He was a Civil War veteran who had commanded an artillery battery in Major General George Crook's Second Division in the Appomattox Campaign. His new position was a responsible one involving expenditures of $100,000 to $150,000 or more per year, even though the depot's most active years had passed with the Indian wars.[11] He certainly had sufficient influence to find his young nephew a steady occupation. After recovering his health under the care of his uncle and aunt, Russel Tracy found himself appointed military storekeeper of Cheyenne Depot.

Fort Russell was established July 21, 1867, a year before the Union Pacific Railroad's arrival, to protect the construction crews. Due to its central location at the base of the Rockies and three miles west of Cheyenne, the Army decided to make it a permanent post. For similar reasons, Captain Elias B. Carlin in August located a site for a depot halfway between Cheyenne and Fort Russell on the latter's military reserve. The Army intended to make use of the newly available rail transport from the East, and Cheyenne was the logical distribution point. Camp Carlin soon grew into the second largest military depot in the nation, supplying ten to fifteen different western military posts. On its grounds were sixteen large warehouses arranged along two railroad sidings, offices and quarters, and many workshops for wheelwrights, blacksmiths, carpenters, and saddle and harness makers. Large corrals and stables normally held at least 1,000 mules. Some 100 wagons and 5 pack trains were available for shipping.

The depot's principal function was handling wagon

transport to the posts it served. Indian annuity goods for a number of reservations were also distributed. Business was particularly active during the Plains Indian wars of the 1870s as numerous military expeditions were outfitted at Cheyenne. The depot performed this role for the last time in 1879, outfitting General Crook's relief of Major Thomas T. Thornburgh's troops who had had a disastrous encounter with Utes near Meeker, Colorado. At its height, from 500 to 1,000 civilian employees worked at the post. During the 1880s when Tracy was there the figure was closer to 300.[12] There were others besides Tracy who used these jobs to launch successful careers. Caleb Perry Organ arrived in Cheyenne in October 1867 as an ordinary mule skinner but later became general superintendent of Cheyenne Depot. From there he moved on to prosperity as a cattleman and merchant. As a Cheyenne hardware merchant, he had branch stores in Douglas and Buffalo, served one term in 1888 in the upper house of the legislature, and ran the same year on the Democratic ticket for territorial delegate, a contest he lost to Republican Joseph M. Carey.[13]

In 1880 the military was the number one "export industry" in Wyoming. Over the next decade its importance declined, but it remained one of the top four basic industries, trailing railroading and hauling, stock raising, and mining with 14.5 percent of Wyoming's work force engaged as military servicemen. The only higher percentages were those in "general and crop agriculture" (15.4 percent) and unspecified laborers (17.4 percent). Compared with the percentage of the nation as a whole, 96.6 times as many persons were military servicemen in Wyoming. The military income in Wyoming played a significant role in stimulating its economy and in providing the means to build towns like Cheyenne. Fort

Russell, housing one of the larger garrisons, was an important contributor to these figures. Cheyenne Depot, because only a handful of troops was normally stationed there, was not, but the flow of income that maintained these servicemen and all their accountrements and equipment is best represented by the depot that sat at the hub of the whole process. Moreover, the depot, through the civilians it hired and the contracts it let, stimulated a whole range of local industries even more directly than the military as a whole.[14]

Tracy remembers his job of military storekeeper as "not heavy but interesting. I received and had charge of all Government property and shipped it, upon requisition, to the various forts in Wyoming, Idaho, Colorado, Arizona and other forts in the Department of the Platte....It was my responsibility to select the equipment for all Government expeditions leaving Cheyenne Depot or that vicinity." This work could have unexpected complications:

> On one occasion I received some 500 mules from Missouri, each one of which I had to describe, giving its color, markings, height, weight, approximate age and name. This description of the mules was carried on all Government records wherever they went in order to identify them, until such time as they were inspected, condemned and branded with an "I.C."
>
> It was no easy matter to secure names for such a number, but I was assisted in this frequently by teamsters and pack masters. For example, one Mr. Monday who drove a six-mule team suggested the names of Tuesday, Wednesday, Thursday, Friday, Saturday, and Sunday. Others suggested the months of the year, the twelve Apostles, and the names of most of our political leaders or politicians.
>
> One teamster who claimed he had the most vicious, deceptive, and ungovernable mules in the corral promised

> to visit the most notorious and disreputable "sporting house" in Cheyenne and secure appropriate names.[15]

It is not known how much Tracy was paid for these duties, but teamsters at the post earned $35 a month and the quartermaster's chief clerk received $150 a month.[16] It can be assumed that the military storekeeper's salary was toward the upper end of this range.

Although the Indian wars were all but over by Tracy's arrival, many famous Army participants still passed through Cheyenne, where Tracy had the opportunity to outfit, meet, and travel with them. The President's 1883 party may have been the most elaborate expedition Tracy ever furnished, but the 1881 trip with General Sheridan into Yellowstone by way of the Big Horn Mountains was doubtless the most exciting. Major Lord also introduced Tracy to General Oliver Otis Howard and General George Crook. The latter, who still had one Indian war—the one involving Geronimo—to complete, was in the habit of making a long fall hunt annually, usually outfitting at Cheyenne Depot. In 1881 Tracy and his uncle accompanied Crook on such a hunt into the Medicine Bow country of south central Wyoming. According to Crook's biographer, the general was not particularly lively company but was an unparalleled outdoorsman:

> General Crook takes his cup of coffee, soaks in it a handful of hardtack, retires to a nook, sits down, and gets through his meal in silence. He is remarkably abstemious, rarely drinks coffee or tea, except when on a trip in the mountains, can scarcely ever be prevailed upon to touch whiskey, and then never more than a spoonful—in brief he is the most abstemious man I have ever been associated with.
>
> We have no books with us this time, but to him the

> great book of nature lies always open. He knows the course of rivers and the trend of mountains as if by instinct, and can find his way through dark and tangled forests with the certainty of an aborigine. If there is any game near, his keen eye detects its track, his steady foot follows it, and his unerring rifle brings it down. If the stream on which we camp is trout-bearing, his skill as a fisherman will lure the finny tribe where all others fail.

The twenty-one-year-old Tracy shared this high opinion of Crook. He killed a grizzly on this hunt by following the general's advice of always "shooting the bear in the shoulder thus breaking him down so he could not run, then killing him with two or three shots required."[17]

On this same trip he and Major Lord watched a struggle between the bull leaders of two herds of six hundred-plus elk:

> As these great elk approached with lowered antlers, they plowed the earth and threw great clouds of dust over their backs. When within thirty yards they rushed at each other with tremendous force, the impact causing a report like a sledge hammer on an anvil, and which could have been heard for miles away.
>
> As the fight progressed their hoofs were pressed deep in the sand, their backs were bowed, it was a cold day and their breath poured from their nostrils like steam from a pipe, their tongues protruded six or eight inches. At times they became exhausted and with horns interlocked they fell upon their shoulders while their hind feet remained upon the ground. As they rested like gladiators, for a few minutes, their strength returned and they renewed the fight until a prong was broken and they were up fighting again, each straining and struggling, knowing that as the result of that battle one would be recognized as the leader and champion of the entire united herd while the defeated one would be driven away alone into the mountains

where he would not be recognized as a leader or champion by either cow or calf.[18]

After this battle ended, Tracy and Lord each shot a large trophy elk, and Tracy displayed his antlers and the grizzly's skin on the wall of the Tracy Club in later years.

The West had obviously been good for Tracy, and except for one minor relapse he seems to have gained strength in the mountain air. He took trips into the Colorado mountains with his sister and visiting friends from back East. He went hunting with his uncle. A photograph taken in 1881 shows him very much the cowboy, perhaps even the Virginian, that product of Owen Wister's easterner imagination. Looking steely-eyed and ready for action, Russel stands with his right hand on a revolver stuck through a gun belt. His left hand holds the barrel of a single-shot rifle, perhaps the .45-.90 with which he killed his elk. He wears a low-crowned, wide-brimmed, white hat, a double-breasted dark shirt, denim trousers, and a scarf around his neck. On his boots are spurs, and a loyal hound lies at his feet. Undoubtedly Tracy was posing a bit for the folks back home but not as a storekeeper. It is clear that he was responding romantically to the West.

One way to increase his stake in the region was Tracy's investment in its continued growth. His relatives in Mansfield, Ohio, had loaned their capital on mortgages, a popular investment among prosperous easterners. Tracy would also have seen it as a logical investment. Although the precise date of his first venture is unknown, by 1884, the $2000 legacy had been lent out in mortgages of five, seven, and nine hundred dollars, investments that no doubt furnished sound conversation for the visit to Yellowstone with his father and three friends that same year. It was a pleasant and adventurous journey, enlivened by an incident between the eastern guests and a less domesticated western paper. After reaching Beaver Canyon and obtaining buckboard and saddle horses, the Tracy party was ready to head into the park, when "a typical westerner of frontier days" asked them to share a drink:

> These gentlemen were Deacons in the churches at home [Ohio] and were horrified at even the sight of liquor.
>
> This incensed the rancher, who was dolled to attract attention with an old ten-gallon hat trimmed with a 'coon skin, a red bandanna around his neck, boots, and spurs. He had a belt full of cartridges and a six-shooter strapped to his belt. Notwithstanding, he went to his buckboard for his shotgun, and began shooting in the air.
>
> Our party feared trouble and started on our way to the Yellowstone, each one in the party urging the other to hurry on. But when we reached the mouth of the canyon we found that this ranchman had anticipated us and reached there by a short-cut. He had parked his wagon in the middle of the road, making it impossible for us to move forward or turn backward.
>
> He fired a few shots into the air and then approached us, saying to my father, "Now, you G___ d___ dudes, I will see if you will insult a westerner by refusing to drink with him."
>
> My father's hand was trembling almost as much at the thought of taking liquor as at the thought of taking the bullet. I reached out my hand and took the bottle from him and remarked to the ranchman, "Don't waste good liquor on this bunch; they don't know what's good. Let me have it." I then pressed a few drops to my lips and allowed the balance to run down my sleeve until the ranchman, who was so drunk he could hardly see, was reasonably satisfied and allowed us to go on.
>
> As we hurried on through the canyon preceding the ranchman, my guests kept looking backward continuously and remarked, "We have heard much of the wild

> and woolly West but we never expected to be received in this manner.[19]

Everyone seems to have accepted young Tracy's lack of abstemiousness calmly, and apparently this encounter with unsavory western customs—alarming while it happened but no doubt the centerpiece of many a dinner table conversation afterwards—did not diminish the Ohioans' delight in Yellowstone itself. When the geyser then known as Old Phil Sheridan or Hell's Half Acre erupted, it created "a column of boiling, steaming water the size of the Hotel Utah, possibly even greater in height, churning before [us]." His father, moved to tears, exclaimed, "Oh, my boy, why did you not tell me so I could have brought all the family." Whether the Ohioans were impressed with the country, by their guide, or by a combination, they decided to stake some of their money on Russel Tracy and the West. They thereby planted seeds which Tracy-Collins Bank and Trust and its investors, clients, and customers harvest today. Tracy described the decision, made on their return from Yellowstone, simply:

> It was . . . while discussing business and mortgage loans . . . that I conceived the idea of selling to them the mortgages I then held . . . representing my entire savings. The proceeds were reinvested in other mortgages, thus replenishing my stock. Since then we have continued to sell to these gentlemen, their children and grandchildren.[20]

Young Tracy thus was shifting gears. Instead of merely using his capital for an occasional mortgage investment, he was entering a new career as a full-time mortgage broker. He could lend $500 on a house at more than 10 percent, possibly as much as 12 or 15 percent. If he then sold the mortgage to friends in Mansfield at half or less of the interest he collected, he stood to make large profits. Because of the great demand for money in

Cheyenne, people would accept such terms, and Tracy had practically a wide-open field for growth.

Russel did not identify the three Ohio gentlemen by name, but at least one of them was a member of the family which ran the Wagner Hardware Company, possibly C. C. Wagner, who during a later purchase of Tracy Company stock, mentioned "the family loyalty to you and your institution (for over thirty years)." Other Mansfield clients and thus possibly members of the Yellowstone party were G. W. Blymyer, Jr., of the Blymyer Brothers Company, and J. B. Lindley. Much of the success of western mortgage companies in the late nineteenth-century depended on their ability to tap such eastern connections. The competition for investors was keen.[21]

Tracy always attributed much of his success to his three "charter" investors:

> From these gentlemen (financiers of the old school) I received valuable advice and suggestions, which I adopted and which were largely responsible for the methods and practices which have since characterized the business in this company.
>
> In the beginning I decided that my motto should be "Not the most, but safest loans," and resolved that my first aim should be that every client must be absolutely protected, and second, that each must be perfectly satisfied.[22]

In 1884 Cheyenne seemed a good bet for starting a financial institution. The Wyoming range was overflowing with cattle; from 450,000 in 1879, the number had risen to 1.5 million in 1885. Cattlemen had inexpensively driven large herds north from Texas. The half-wild animals seemed to thrive on the northern bunch grass, and they multiplied rapidly. Each fall they were released to fend for themselves on Wyoming's open range and each spring they were rounded up and shipped to Omaha or Chicago. Prices in Chicago markets climbed steadily from 1881 through 1884, and soon everyone from Scottish gentry to Texas drifters wanted a piece of the action. Eastern and overseas capital also flowed into the territory, either through direct investment in cattle companies or through the extension of the credit so necessary to a business as seasonal as this. Recognizing the "bonanza" of not having to buy land or feed, the British are said to have put $45 million into American cattle during the 1880s.[23]

Cheyenne was a major beneficiary of these conditions, its railroad link with the eastern markets making the boom possible. True, the eastern capital that followed improved links with this previously isolated western region sometimes threatened to squeeze out the local entrepreneur. But in the early 1880s there seemed room for all. In 1884 there were four banks in Cheyenne serving a population approaching six thousand people. Two were national—First National and Stockgrowers' National—and two were private—Morton E. Post & Co. and T. A. Kent.[24] Easterners often funneled their money into the West through local loan agencies or commission firms. During the horrendous winter of 1886-87 the cattle carcasses that had piled up by spring demonstrated graphically the weaknesses in a system which allowed cattle to roam untended during the worst part of the year. Some estimates placed livestock losses as high as 75 percent. More careful modern analysis concludes that Wyoming lost closer to 15 percent and Laramie County only 5 percent.

Cheyenne had enough momentum in 1887 to drive on after the boom collapsed. Major developments in that single year including the building of the Cheyenne and Burlington Railroad and purchase of depot and real estate by the company amounting to half a million dollars; the erection of the territorial capitol building at a cost of $300,000; the 125-mile extension of the Cheyenne and Northern Railway to the Platte River; the building of a $100,000 depot by the Union Pacific Railroad; the letting of a contract for erecting buildings at Fort Russell in the amount of $50,000; and the construction of a handsome stone Episcopal church at a cost of $40,000. In that year also a free mail delivery system was established; a territorial blind, deaf, and dumb asylum was erected; the territorial fairgrounds were completed; a street railway line was built; the city park was improved; fifty "palatial" residences were built; and half a dozen additions to the city were laid out.[25]

It is unlikely that Tracy's institution made many loans on the cattle range, although the livestock industry indirectly contributed to his business by helping stimulate more general growth. Tracy's initial loans were comparatively small; and ranchers, who preferred the free range to buying land, were more likely to use their livestock than land for collateral. Although cattlemen were beginning to file on public lands in the early 1880s, few of these entries led to patents.[26] Tracy thus lent almost exclusively on improved farms and city residences.

As new railroads were constructed in Wyoming in the 1880s, more settlers came into the territory to compete with the cattle industry. Farming made considerable gains, especially after the cattle industry went into a tailspin in the last half of the decade. Among other places, farmers moved into the Goshen Hole area north of Cheyenne to plant wheat. According to the census the number of those engaged in general and crop agriculture

CHAPTER 2

# Successful Transplant to Utah: 1892-1902

Russel Tracy had visited Salt Lake City regularly since 1885 before transferring his business there. He had become aware that sluggish economic conditions as well as Cheyenne's small size made it impossible for him, as he put it, to find "enough satisfactory securities to fill the demand I had even then from my eastern clients."[1] Satisfactory may be translated as *safe*, something any investor in Cheyenne's roller-coaster economy had to look hard to find. Cheyenne's 1890 population had climbed to 11,690 but Salt Lake City had 44,843 inhabitants, up from 20,768 in 1880. To this could be added an increasingly urbanized population all along the Wasatch Front, where more than 75,000 persons had located. This was the kind of pool Tracy needed to get his young business securely on its feet. He was having no trouble finding investors—his eastern connections were paying off—but a growing urban area, especially one surrounded by industrious farmers and artisans, ought to provide the necessary borrowers as well.

In 1885, on an early trip, he wrote a description of his Ogden to Denver train ride on the Denver & Rio Grande Western Railroad which was published in his hometown newspaper at Mansfield, Ohio. By coincidence the engine pulling this train was No. 223, later on display in Liberty Park next to the aviary which Tracy donated to Salt Lake City. Tracy wrote eloquently of the northern Utah landscape:

> It is a beautiful country, with flowers in full bloom, apple and peach trees in blossom, and clover several inches high. Apparently within a few yards a background of mountains perfectly white with snow. Now all is warm; windows open and the fragrance from the fields speak in no mistaken terms of summer. A few hours later we are slowly but surely climbing the mountains. The windows one after another are closed; the green fields and blooming trees are all below us; the people on the platform come in; the porter builds a fire; and now snow and ice form the bed over which we ride.[2]

In 1892, he decided to make the move, transferring both his business and his residence to Salt Lake City. Behind in Cheyenne he left a trusted associate, Albert Chapman, to collect and remit the proceeds from his Wyoming mortgages. Chapman continued to run the business as an investment, insurance, and real estate enterprise for some years. He then passed it on to his son Mark who operated it well into the twentieth century.

In the short run, it was not an auspicious move; Salt Lake City would be hit just as hard as Cheyenne by the Panic of 1893. In the long-run, though, it promised greater opportunity because of its steady growth. During previous visits, Tracy had made some good friends, and "the whole atmosphere of Salt Lake was attuned with his high regard for the people."[3] By the turn of the century both Utah and Russel Tracy's company had entered a period of solid progress.

Since its settlement in 1847 Salt Lake City and Utah had struggled through at least two distinct stages in their economic growth. Mormon leader Brigham Young had encouraged an economic policy of self-sufficiency. During the first two decades of settlement in the isolated Great Basin, such a policy reflected necessity as well as religious ideology. Having fled mob persecution in Ohio, Missouri, and Illinois, Mormon pioneers understandably felt a certain desire to draw inward and sever dependencies on a hostile United States. Moreover, the cost of importing goods across the long miles between Utah and the Missouri frontier provided additional incentive for growing and making necessities at home. The cost of freighting could raise the price of as simple a necessity as nails, for example, from 10¢ a pound in Atchison to $1.30 a pound in Salt Lake City.[4]

First priority to the new settlers was feeding themselves and the thousands of immigrants gathering each year to their valley. In consequence, the Great Basin, one of the most arid regions in North America, became a crop producer. Since midwestern agriculture was not particularly suitable to the arid mountain valleys, farmers depended on the development of irrigation, cooperative labor, and church-supported manufacturing enterprises to survive. Mormon leaders campaigned incessantly for the establishment of tanneries, wool and cotton factories, iron foundries, salt and sugar refineries, and even some mining. Church-directed colonizing missions were sent to Cedar City to mine iron and to Las Vegas to mine lead. Some lucky breaks came to the struggling settlements in the form of forty-niners headed for California, who traded or abandoned their surplus goods or restocked with necessities at Salt Lake City. Later, a large force of United States troops was stationed at Camp Floyd, Utah; their quartermasters purchased local products and later, when they were recalled east to fight in the Civil War, some for the North and some for the South, they sold to Utahns millions of dollars of supplies and equipment at bargain basement prices.[5]

Although this "ecclesiastical commonwealth" reached a certain level of self-sufficiency, it was never as independent of outside economic forces or as free of outsiders as it set out to be. As mining districts opened up across the West, Utah farms became something of a breadbasket for the camps. But since church leaders generally discouraged Mormon prospecting, especially for gold and silver, most was done by non-Mormons—often referred to at the time as "gentiles." Troops stationed at Fort Douglas on Salt Lake City's eastern foothills after 1862 were encouraged by their virulently anti-Mormon commandant, Colonel Patrick E. Connor, to prospect in their spare time. Connor hoped to create a "miner's rush" of non-Mormons to the community, thus diluting the power of the Mormon leadership. By the end of the 1860s, gold and silver mines were operating at several locations in the Wasatch and Oquirrh Mountains.

Since, in the cause of self-sufficiency, Latter-day Saints were discouraged from buying what they could not produce themselves, the importation of retail goods was another activity which came to be dominated by non-Mormons. By the time the transcontinental railroad arrived in 1869, permanently altering Utah's isolation, two separate and rather hostile economies had developed.

in Wyoming increased from 1,364 to 3,784 during the 1880s. Although this represents a significant increase, Wyoming was still a cattle state. Those in stock-raising increased from 275 to 4,147 over the same decade.[27] If Tracy's first loans are translated into acres at the rate of $2.50 per acre (the standard rate for a railroad grant corridor like Cheyenne) they could have financed land purchases of 200, 280, and 320 acres. Again, though, judging by later practice, Tracy would have taken mortgages only on more valuable patented or at least improved lots and certainly at no more than 50 percent of their assessed value.

Thus, while it is difficult to identify specific loans, it is clear that Tracy's business rode the general wave of Cheyenne's prosperity in the early 1880s. As military storekeeper at Camp Carlin, he was able to keep attuned to business conditions in the city and make contacts with potential customers. He was still working there in 1885 and his uncle was present in May 1890 when the depot was dismantled and the buildings sold and either destroyed or moved. But Russel was no longer on the payroll.[28]

Meanwhile, the young entrepreneur was conducting a profitable business from a downtown office. A 1940s Cheyenne newspaper article described it as a "flimsy frame building, hardly more than a shack.... This stood about where... the north end of the Shapiro building" later stood. To attract eastern capital, Tracy is said to have distributed an album of steel engravings of Cheyenne's more important buildings, done from photographs by C. D. Kirkland.[29]

His business was only three years old in 1887 when Cheyenne's economy floundered and failed. The cattle that had survived the winter were in very poor condition and brought little on the market, glutted with animals, both from other areas and from the northern plains where debt-ridden owners tried to get out from under the winter's losses. The newly arrived Episcopal bishop, who came expecting to find "the richest town of its size in the whole world to-day," described the conditions he found:

> So profitable had the cattle interest become that those engaged in it had felt justified in investing all they had in that business, and also in mortgaging their credit to the uttermost limit and going heavily in debt. The result was that, when the crisis came, not only were the cattle gone, but large liabilities and no assets wherewith to meet them faced those who had counted their wealth by hundreds of thousands and even millions. It took years for Wyoming to recover from the wide-spread and desolating losses then incurred, and the depression of feeling resting upon the little city of Cheyenne at the time of my first visit was pathetically evident.[30]

Farmers benefited somewhat from the reduction in competition by cattlemen for land, and there was some increase in post-1886 farming in Laramie County and elsewhere. However, the 1880s boom in agriculture on the Plains stopped short of Wyoming. One historian has noted that while "people swarmed into western Nebraska in the years 1885-1890, . . . only a few thousand crossed into Wyoming." The main beneficiaries of few cattle on the range were sheepmen, not farmers.[31]

Three Wyoming banks closed during the depression of the late 1880s, including Morton E. Posts's in Cheyenne. A fledgling business like Russel Tracy's must have looked very vulnerable, but it survived. Apparently his commitment to safe loans had served him well, as it would in later periods of financial panic and economic crisis.

Cheyenne recovered slowly, and there was even a

brief revival of investment in cattle between 1889 and 1891, but the Cheyenne National Bank failed in November 1891. However, compared with other western states, Wyoming's growth was sluggish. Even in prosperity of the early 1880s, Wyoming's population growth trailed Idaho and Montana. When the "Cleveland Panic" of 1893 hit, all of the West felt the pain, but Cheyenne, which was still shaking off its earlier problems, was especially hurt. T. A. Kent and First National Bank both closed their doors in July 1893.[32] Other financial institutions came close to the same fate, but Russel L. Tracy was not one of them. The previous year he had decided to move to the presumably greener pastures of Salt Lake City, Utah.

by industrious farmers and artisans, ought to provide the necessary borrowers as well.

In 1885, on an early trip, he wrote a description of his Ogden to Denver train ride on the Denver & Rio Grande Western Railroad which was published in his hometown newspaper at Mansfield, Ohio. By coincidence the engine pulling this train was No. 223, later on display in Liberty Park next to the aviary which Tracy donated to Salt Lake City. Tracy wrote eloquently of the northern Utah landscape:

> It is a beautiful country, with flowers in full bloom, apple and peach trees in blossom, and clover several inches high. Apparently within a few yards a background of mountains perfectly white with snow. Now all is warm; windows open and the fragrance from the fields speak in no mistaken terms of summer. A few hours later we are slowly but surely climbing the mountains. The windows one after another are closed; the green fields and blooming trees are all below us; the people on the platform come in; the porter builds a fire; and now snow and ice form the bed over which we ride.[2]

In 1892, he decided to make the move, transferring both his business and his residence to Salt Lake City. Behind in Cheyenne he left a trusted associate, Albert Chapman, to collect and remit the proceeds from his Wyoming mortgages. Chapman continued to run the business as an investment, insurance, and real estate enterprise for some years. He then passed it on to his son Mark who operated it well into the twentieth century.

In the short run, it was not an auspicious move; Salt Lake City would be hit just as hard as Cheyenne by the Panic of 1893. In the long-run, though, it promised greater opportunity because of its steady growth. During previous visits, Tracy had made some good friends, and

CHAPTER 2

# Successful Transplant to Utah: 1892-1902

Russel Tracy had visited Salt Lake City regularly since 1885 before transferring his business there. He had become aware that sluggish economic conditions as well as Cheyenne's small size made it impossible for him, as he put it, to find "enough satisfactory securities to fill the demand I had even then from my eastern clients."[1] Satisfactory may be translated as *safe*, something any investor in Cheyenne's roller-coaster economy had to look hard to find. Cheyenne's 1890 population had climbed to 11,690 but Salt Lake City had 44,843 inhabitants, up from 20,768 in 1880. To this could be added an increasingly urbanized population all along the Wasatch Front, where more than 75,000 persons had located. This was the kind of pool Tracy needed to get his young business securely on its feet. He was having no trouble finding investors—his eastern connections were paying off—but a growing urban area, especially one surrounded

Standing opposed to the Mormon family-and church-oriented village society which continued to experiment with self-sufficient communitarian or cooperative organizations such as Zion's Co-operative Mercantile Institution and the United Order, were unruly and transitory mining camps, largely fueled by speculative eastern and midwestern capital. Both economies were headquartered in and serviced by Salt Lake City. As Utah over the next two to three decades became a mining as well as agricultural territory, so Salt Lake City, with improved communication and transportation links, became, in addition to the capital of a cooperative religious commonwealth, the nexus for commerce throughout the Mountain West. Parallel with the increased economic activity, financial institutions evolved to meet the need for money and banking.

Utah banking also grew out of separate Mormon and non-Mormon activities. Most financial services during the early years of settlement were provided by either centralized church institutions or by merchants. The church's banking practices were initially the most extensive because of the heavy Mormon population. They included the introduction of coin and currency to supplement other circulating media, the provision of short-term consumer and commercial credit through the same agencies and the church treasury, and the handling of drafts, remittances, and other "foreign" credit instruments through the agency of such church institutions as the Perpetual Emigrating Fund Company. A particularly serious problem in the region was the shortage of money. Several times between 1847 and 1860, Mormon leaders addressed this need by minting coin from California gold brought to Utah or printing currency backed by gold or church-owned livestock.

Tithing houses located in every Mormon village were clearinghouses for community trade and commerce. Usually serving as the only general store in town, they kept track, through extensive bookkeeping, of each individual's deposits in produce at the community storehouse and animals in the community livestock herd. Records of each customer's debits and credits were maintained, and thereby community members were in effect borrowing and saving. The tithing houses also issued tithing scrip which circulated throughout most of the territory as a form of currency.

Just as many of the tithing office's banking functions grew out of their general store activities, so did Mormon and non-Mormon merchants, as a natural extension of running their business, assume the role which banks played elsewhere. A fundamental service in a money-short community was to allow the purchase of goods on credit. Early mercantile establishments like Livingston, Kinkead and Bell; Holladay and Warner; John and Enoch Reese; Andrew and Levi Stewart; J. M. Horner; and J. M. Hockaday went well beyond this. Because they had strong vaults, they allowed customers to leave money on deposit and issued receipts much like bankers' certificates of deposit. They were in the business of buying and selling, and they included gold dust and drafts on eastern banks as well as merchandise among their transactions. They also worked as a clearinghouse for their customers by accepting promissory notes drawn between them and transferring the transaction between the accounts of the individuals.[7]

Mining created a need for more formal banking institutions. Miners, mining companies, and the merchants and freighters who served them needed a place where they could sell or store their gold, have it transferred to the East or San Francisco, deposit savings, profits, and payrolls, and get loans. Salt Lake City, with an established population and business community, was centrally located to serve not only Utah but new mining districts in eastern Nevada, Idaho, and Montana. By 1864, the need was sufficient to attract Salt Lake City's first licensed bank, Clark and Company, soon followed by Holladay and Halsey run by Ben Holladay of Overland Mail fame.[8] Both grew out of mercantile and freighting operations.

These and other early private banks were opportune enterprises whose founders sought to meet the financial needs of the new mines in addition to engaging in other commercial activities. They were unregulated, had no capital of their own, and offered minimal protection for customers' deposits. Banking though, entered a new, more sophisticated phase with the passage of the National Banking Act in 1863 (revised in 1864). This allowed the establishment of national banks, primarily in order to regularize national currency through the issuance of national bank notes backed by government bonds deposited with the newly created Comptroller of the Currency in Washington, D. C. National banks were required to have a substantial paid-up capital ($100,000 for cities the size of Salt Lake City) and to maintain a 15 percent reserve against notes and deposits. They were prohibited from making loans on real estate or the security of the bank's own stock. The comptroller chartered, supervised, and examined them.[9]

Miner's National Bank with a capital of $150,000 received a charter in 1866 as Utah's first national bank. The First National Bank of Utah and the Salt Lake City National Bank soon followed. But the most important and longest enduring of these early national banks was the Deseret National Bank established in 1872 by William Hooper, Horace Eldredge, and Lewis Hills, prominent Mormon merchants. Although ostensibly independent, the bank was seen as an official Mormon Church business. Brigham Young was its president, and its initial name was Zion's Co-operative Banking Institution. It consequently gained a lion's share of the Mormon community's business. The other exception to the rule of banks founded by non-Mormon merchants for the needs of miners was a stepchild of Deseret National, Zion's Savings Bank & Trust Company, which in 1873 took over the savings department of Deseret National. When the Panic of 1873 crippled the mining industry, the other national banks discontinued business, but Deseret National, relying on the more self-sufficient and stable Mormon economy, survived.

Besides the national banks, many territorially chartered and private banks were founded between the 1860s and 1890s. Most came and went at a shocking rate. Of fifty-four banks established between 1864 and 1887, thirty-seven did not survive.[10] Exceptions were three important private banks that lasted into the twentieth century: W. S. McCornick and Company, for many years Utah's largest private bank with deposits in 1900 of $5 million; Wells, Fargo, and Company, heir to Ben Holladay's interests; and Walker Brothers Bank, which began as part of one of Salt Lake City's oldest and largest mercantile businesses and eventually bought out the other two.

During the 1870s and 1880s, there continued to be a close connection between mining and banking activity in Utah. Allowing for a one-year lag, the number of banks demonstrated close correlation with the value of minerals produced. Since this was a time of erratic overnight booms and busts in the mineral industry, it is no wonder that many banks had little staying power. After 1885, the correlation was less close, an indication that banks were serving a broader clientele.[11] Utah's economy was changing. Mining remained extremely important, but easily worked surface ores were largely gone. More stable, highly organized, and capital-intensive companies were necessary to mine the low-grade ores at deeper levels. During the 1890s, mineral production maintained more stable levels.

Livestock-raising became a major industry during the last two decades of the nineteenth century, helping to diversify Utah's agricultural base. New manufactures also began to appear. Particularly significant was the increase in commercial activity in Salt Lake City, as new hotels, retail outlets, and other businesses popped up in the increasingly cosmopolitan business district. The real-estate business grew, reflecting the boom in commercial and residential building. Mining profits were poured into ostentatious mansions along South Temple Street and new subdivisions opened throughout the city. Between 1874 and 1896, real estate businesses increased from four to sixty-eight firms.[12]

Banks grew in numbers and deposits as well. The greatest growth was between 1888 and 1892 when thirty-four new banks opened in Utah. Most of the new banks in the last two decades of the nineteenth century were established outside of Salt Lake City, demonstrating that economic growth was spreading into the countryside.[13] Utah's first significant banking act was passed in 1888 by the territorial legislature. It was the basis of all later efforts to regulate banking within the territory and state. It set limits on the amount of capitalization necessary to establish a bank—$25,000 to $1 million depending on the size of the town where the bank was located. The law also required six or more persons to incorporate a bank, two-thirds of whom had to be territorial residents; stipulated that 25 percent of the capital had to be paid in before business commenced; restricted the amount that could be loaned to bank officers; made the secretary of the territory an ex-officio bank examiner who should examine every bank at least once and no more than twice a year; set the liability of stockholders at double the par value of their stock; allowed women and children to make and draw deposits in their own names; required banks to publish quarterly statements; and established other procedures for incorporating. According to one scholar, passage of this act seems to have succeeded in reducing the number of bank failures and creating more stability in Utah's financial community.[14] None of the banks in the territory failed during the Panic of 1893 (two temporarily closed their doors), a fact attributed to "their conservatism... the prudence and coolness of the banking fraternity as well as the unshaken confidence of the masses of the people of the state." Local banks had anticipated and prepared for the trouble, months before it came. Their principal salvation was due to the light deposits they were carrying when the panic came.[15]

In short, during the years Russel Tracy was becoming established in Salt Lake City, the region was going through significant social and economic change. The perennial conflict between the Mormon Church and the federal government was cooling off, the Congress and the President agreed to grant statehood to Utah in 1896.

Thus, when Russel Tracy went to Salt Lake City in 1892, the Mormon Zion was entering into a new era in which two differing economies were merged with each other, and there was greater diversification and commercialization. Tracy was an active proponent of this bridging of the two ways of life and was well accepted by both the Mormon and the "gentile" communities. He was a force for toleration, harmony, and reconcilation.[16]

Although it was the direct ancestor of Tracy-Collins Bank and Trust, Russel Tracy's early financial operation in Wyoming and Salt Lake City did not, by some criteria, qualify as a bank. He did not take deposits, issue bank notes, or offer a full range of credit services. The bank examiner did not include his company under the list of operating banks. When he incorporated, ten years after the move to Salt Lake City, Tracy described his company as "a general loan, brokerage and commission business."[17] The evolution of Tracy's initial mortgage loan company into a full-service commercial bank was gradual. It had its roots in the Salt Lake mortgage boom that began with the 1870 completion of the Utah Central Railroad, which connected Salt Lake City with the Union Pacific and Central Pacific junction at Ogden, and continued into the 1870s, 1880s, and 1890s. New settlers needed cash to buy land, build homes and outbuildings, dig wells, and build fences. Speculators betting on the continued increase in Wasatch Front land values also needed capital, preferably someone else's. Small businessmen depended on credit to get on their feet.[18]

Both the High Country of Wyoming and the Great Basin region may have been chronically short of money, but the value of the land itself was a compensation. As settlement continued in the Mountain West, land promised to appreciate in value. It was, then, a seemingly ideal security for the investor. Moreover, the demand for credit kept interest rates high. Usury laws provided some restraint, but there were various ways around them, especially through the commissions and fees charged by agents negotiating the loans. The potential profits which may have attracted an enterprising young Westerner are evident if it is assumed that he loaned money at 7 1/2 percent, returning 6 percent to his investors and keeping 1 1/2 percent as his profit. These were in fact the national averages in 1890, but the figures were several points higher in the mountain states and territories.

> A mortgage company . . . first loans out its own capital at an average net rate of 7 1/2%, then it sells debentures [or the mortgages themselves], and loans out again the money received from the sale of these debentures. A company that, for the sake of illustration, can loan every year only twice the amount of its own capital stock, and can at the same time keep its own capital permanently invested in mortgages, earns twice 1 1/2% or 3%; the average life of the mortgages being nearly five years, this means earnings of five times 3% or 15% plus 7 1/2%, the permanent interest on the invested capital stock, or 22 1/2% per annum.[19]

Tracy sold completed mortgages rather than debentures—bonds secured by mortgages deposited with a trustee—but this process was in essence the basis of his profits.

High interest rates and the apparent safety of investment in land had brought a flood of outside capital into the Mountain West, which crested in the mid-1880s when Russel Tracy was just entering the business in Cheyenne. Funds came from a wide spectrum of eastern investors. Insurance companies were among the largest suppliers of capital, but individual capitalists and small businessmen were active as well. One estimate placed the annual volume of western mortgage business at the end of the 1880s near $150 million.[20] In every small town in the West, local agents sprang up to recruit borrowers and negotiate the transactions. Often they were lawyers or small businessmen who garnered loan commissions on the side and gradually, depending on the amount of local borrowing, devoted more of their time to mortgages.

Western mortgages generally required three participants: the eastern investor, the Western borrower, and the agent, broker, or banker in the middle. The role of the borrower as mortgagor was fairly constant: his land was the security and his needs were the reason for the loan. The role of the other two parties varied considerably, even to the extent of who was technically the mortgagee. Some large investors actively supervised and directed the lending of their capital, even visiting and personally inspecting prospective securities. They employed local agents who received a small commission for their services. As the boom grew, fewer and fewer investors desired or could afford to take such an active interest. They relied on brokers, who circulated in both the East and the West, to find suitable mortgages. Some such brokers evolved into large concerns that completely relieved investors of the bother of supervision. Some guaranteed the loans while others began making loans out of their own capital, accumulating a selection which could be offered to investors on demand. With the development of the debenture, eastern capital was no longer applied to a specific loan. Rather it purchased a mortgage company's own bond which was backed by a pool of mortgages.[21]

Although money-lenders, bankers, capitalists, and especially mortgage companies, performed an indispensable and positive function in the settlement and development of the West, they were the targets of criticism when booms fizzled. Good-weather cycles lured the agricultural frontier well beyond its practicable limits. When droughts and bad winters were followed by falling prices for crops, foreclosures mounted. Populists in the High Plains region saw mortgage brokers as agents of a vast conspiracy to deprive farmers of their homes.[22] Less virulent criticisms claimed that mortgages resulted in a net drain on Western capital instead of providing funds for development.[23] However, although some companies had undoubtedly overrecruited loans and had been careless in their selection of securities, they derived little benefit from depressions. Most companies, in fact, failed between 1888 and 1894. Because of foreclosures, they suddenly found themselves in the real estate business when there was little market for land. With their capital thus tied down, many of them were unable to meet their own obligations.

Those who were able to survive, however, faced bright prospects. Russel Tracy's fidelity to conservative business methods, which fully merited the trust of his investors, weathered the 1880s crisis in Wyoming and the 1890s crisis in Salt Lake City without serious losses. More than two decades after his move to Utah he could advertise that his business had been conducted "without loss to any one purchasing our securities" and "with only one foreclosure" since 1892.[24]

The real-estate loan business, like other aspects of banking, developed more slowly in Salt Lake City than on the Great Plains. Until 1869, when Congress provided for a land office or means to acquire title to public lands, land was distributed to Mormon settlers by the Church surveyor and local bishops. In exchange, the farmers contributed labor to community projects. With no capital investment necessary to acquire plots, there was no need to finance the purchase. Mormons could also turn to the tithing office or other Church institutions to obtain credit necessary for improvements. Such a system virtually eliminated speculation but also left little room for private financial institutions.[25]

After 1869, a wide choice of potential creditors gradually became available to the Utahn seeking a mortgage loan. National banks were prohibited from lending on real estate, but territorial and private banks might do so. There were thirty-three in Utah—nine in Salt Lake City—in 1892. Building and loan associations, of which there were five in Salt Lake City in 1892, had also become an important source of credit during the last half of the nineteenth century. Member-owned and -organized, they loaned the savings deposits of members for the purchase and improvement of homes, encouraging both thrift and home ownership. The two largest in Salt Lake City were the National Building and Loan Association, later the Western Loan and Savings Company, with a capital stock of $1.0 million, and Zion's Benefit Building Society, with capital of $1.5 million.[26]

Other creditors, from insurance companies to private individuals, were willing to put their money to work with Utah property owners. However, Russel Tracy's most direct competition was other loan companies. Their character, size, and methods varied widely; and since directories and classified ads listed everything from pawnbrokers and eastern agents to full-fledged mortgage loan companies under "Loans" and "Money to Loan," it is difficult to tell how many were providing the type of service Tracy offered. It is apparent, though, that the market was not yet saturated in 1892. Local money had been unable to satisfy the demand created by Salt Lake City's growth. A real estate spokesman reported at the end of the year,

> At the close of last year there was very little outside money coming in for investment, and in consequence the usual shortage occurred among local people. Now there is a great deal of outside money coming in which is an

> indication of healthy conditions. The local men, however, are saving their money. They apparently have not as much confidence in the city as outsiders. The result is that outsiders are picking up choice mortgage loans at lower rates than ever before. In a few months the local people will wake up to the situation and find it impossible to place their money at 10 and 12 percent, unless they take poorer securities than they are accustomed to.[27]

Tracy was one of the new sources of that confident outside money.

There were some thirty-three providers of loans that were neither banks nor building-and-loan associations listed in the 1891-92 directory. In the statehood year of 1896 there were still thirty-three, although some names were different, including Tracy as a new addition. Those who advertised in 1893 and 1894 when Tracy began using the classifieds included such varied operations as J. K. Shaw offering "$1,000 to $50,000" at "lowest rates" for "1 to 5 Years." The Miller-Hawley Mortgage Company offered large business loans at 7 percent and smaller and residence loans at 8, 9, or 10 percent. A firm with the propitious name of Virtue and Righter loaned "small sums at [a] reasonable rate of interest"; while I. Watters, Broker, advertised "Money to loan on collatearls [sic]. Unredeemed pledges at reduced rates."[28] Few companies advertised solely for mortgages, but a majority appeared to give them first priority. With interest rates continuing to hover near 10 percent in the early 1890s, they offered clear advantages over loans on less promising securities than land.

Despite the variety of credit businesses, some operated much like Tracy's. One, McGurrin and Company, advertised itself as an "Investment Bank" explaining that

> An Investment Bank differs from a Savings Bank in this: The depositor, instead of handing over his money to the

> bank without any security and leaving it under the absolute control of the banker at 4 or 5 percent per annum, goes to the Investment Bank and looks over a list of mortgage securities upon which the Investment Banker has already loaned his money and selects one of such amount and kind as suits him, and this mortgage is then assigned to him and no one else can interfere with it from that time on.

The advantages of such a system over the operations of agents for eastern concerns came from having

> securities ready for investors when they call. Consequently, he can pick the choicest loans, and the investor is not kept waiting. When his money is ready for investment until the "agent" gets a satisfactory "application." The fact that the Investment Banker loans his own money first, will naturally make him more cautious, than if he were loaning someone else's. He attends to all of the details at the time of making the loan and afterward during its existence, and is never free from responsibility until the investor has his money back with the specified interest.[29]

Although he did not call it investment banking and did not yet seek out local investors, Tracy also preferred to offer a selection of pre-existing loans for sale to his eastern clients.

Tracy arrived in Salt Lake City armed with a letter of introduction to Josiah Barnett, cashier of W. S. McCornick and Company's bank. With the first handshake he was making contact with the central pillar of Utah's financial community. The *Tribune* had recently written that

> . . . W. S. McCornick is a gentleman whose banking interests reach to every corner of the Territory. For years the possessor of the finest residence in Salt Lake, he has recently gratified his pride by the erection of the finest business block in the city, at the corner of Main and First South streets. It is not generally known that Mr. McCornick is a Canadian by birth, having been born in

> Ontario in 1837. In 1860 he emigrated to California where for two years he was engaged in ranching enterprises. Like many other men of that day and country, he drifted into Nevada. There he was engaged for eleven years in lumbering and mining industries, his operations covering almost every point of importance in Nevada. Since coming to Salt Lake Mr. McCornick has linked his name with dozens of enterprises of public importance.[30]

McCornick and Company remained one of Utah's largest private (later state) banks until Walker Bank and Trust purchased it in 1921 following the death of its founder. Josiah Barnett was an active member of Salt Lake's business and financial community in his own right. Among other things, he was a director of the Utah Loan and Building Association. What specific aid Barnett provided to Tracy is unknown, but it is clear he was in a position to be helpful, and took a personal interest in his new colleague. Twenty-three years later he was still doing so, as he was the first subscriber to a special issue of stock offered to a select list of the Tracy company's clients.[31]

Tracy may have desired any inside information he could get on Utah's economy since it was already slowing down at the end of 1892, six months before the days of the panic that launched the "Cleveland Depression." The *Tribune*'s annual report on the business situation noted in December that there was not much real estate business. The community was troubled by a hard winter and an uncertain future for silver mining. At the national level nobody seemed to be doing anything to improve the general conditions. Many people were scared, especially since the 1892 election had not been favorable to silver interests. Banks and other local moneylenders were holding on to their money until they saw sure signs that conditions were improving. Meanwhile, more optimistic outside capital was garnering loans at lower rates and having an additional impact on the local economy.

Tracy moved slowly. His first advertisement for loans did not appear until September 28, 1893. Operating out of a friend's office, he advertised "$20,000 to loan without delay on improved or farm property in sums from $200 to $2,000." (Less than a month later he would offer $25,000).[33] Customers were told to "Call mornings on Russel L. Tracy for a few days at office of Frank B. Stephens, Room 47, Commercial Block." Stephens, who had arrived in Salt Lake City early in 1890, was assistant to the United States Attorney for Utah Territory. Tracy's ad offers evidence that in nine years his available capital had increased ten-fold, that he had a fund which compared favorably with what other loan companies offered, and that spending money on impressive offices was a low priority.

Tracy's ad slogans over the next several years give a good sense of his professional values and personal style. From the first he made it clear that he was more than an agent for easterners. He announced, "Money always on hand," ensuring mortgagors that they did not have to wait for the commitment of funds from somewhere else. He frequently advertised that "I loan only my own money" and promised that by working directly with him as the principal, the borrower would "save commission." A third advantage besides "no delay . . . no commissions" was intended for the easily embarrassed; working directly with Tracy as mortgagee meant "no advertising your wants." These arguments must have been appealing since he continued to use the lending of his own money as his main selling point for many years, offering "no eastern company, no third party, no trust deed" and "no commission expense or delay." He also offered to negotiate rates and terms and to provide "special options" suitable to particular needs.

To a certain extent, these advertisements showed a public relations ability to select the most favorable facts. Technically he may have been lending his own money, but he obviously depended on easterners to replenish his supply as it was loaned out. While he may not have charged commissions, the interest charge amounted to the same thing. And at some point, even if after the fact, a third party was indeed involved in the transaction through the purchase of Tracy's mortgage securities, although since Tracy continued to take care of all the administration of the loan, the borrower never dealt directly with the purchaser of his loan. Still, the basic advantages Tracy claimed were real, especially for a public suspicious of eastern capital.

To clients in the East, Tracy offered only the safest mortgages. From the very beginning, he invested in the growth of the city rather than the countryside, although the two were intimately related. It was the city's growing commerce and population that had attracted him, and it was to the city that he eventually donated his philanthropic as well as business energies. Philosophically, he always measured his success by the number of homes provided for young families. His first advertisement announced money to lend "on improved or farm property," but within three weeks he had changed this to "on city property." City residences were not his only business, by any means; but farms and other securities were always a secondary market.

One of the advantages of focusing on the Salt Lake City market for loans was that Tracy could personally examine the property in question, an argument he used tellingly with clients. On his thirtieth business anniversary in 1914, he explained his method in some detail. In all likelihood, it had been his practice all along:

> For thirty years it has been our practice to invest our own money in the best mortgages in the market, confining them to improved income-producing properties in the best sections of the city, or best farming districts, representing not to exceed from 30 per cent of the value of the property, with improvement insured for the amount of the loan. These loans we in turn sell so as to net our clients a slightly lower rate than we receive, and as we depend for our commission or profit upon what we collect as interest during the life of the loan in excess of what we pay our clients, we have both a moral and financial interest in the loan until it is paid. As we always have on hand such mortgages aggregating more than $200,000 in sums of from $300 to $20,000 each, we can fill orders immediately upon receipt of money.
>
> The property securing every loan has been personally visited and examined by either the President or Vice President of this Company; and for thirty years we have not only protected every client against loss, but we have relieved them of the embarrassment of doing business with the mortgagor and of every detail, care, worry and anxiety incident to the investment of money. We guarantee the title to the property, and that the mortgage is a first lien upon same. We see that the taxes and special assessments are promptly paid and insurance renewed at expiration, that interest is collected and always remitted promptly. In fifteen years no client has had occasion to notify us that interest was delinquent. It always reaches them before it is due.[34]

The real estate market continued sluggish through the mid-1890s. In May 1894, a year after the panic, the most significant real estate activity consisted of properties changing hands at reduced rates following foreclosure.[35] Tracy managed to avoid accumulating land, thus tying his capital down and risking the fate of many western companies dragged under by the unexpected transition from credit financier to property manager. However, Tracy may have experienced some difficulty in finding sufficient mortgage business as indicated in early 1894 by branching off into buying and selling "water scrip" and lending money on "city or country warrants, water scrip or like collateral."[36]

Although such diversions did not last long, there is no indication that Tracy lost money on any of them. A good indication is his role that same year in financing construction of the Salt Lake City and County Building, Salt Lake's new Romanesque monument on State Street and 400 South which was completed and dedicated on December 28, 1894. It was an investment that brought him considerable profit—no small achievement considering its problem-plagued beginnings more than three years earlier. The groundbreaking in 1891 had been preceded by several years of false starts. Architects and building sites had changed. Conflicts with contractors and subcontractors had repeatedly snarled activity in a financial tangle. Completion of the structure was fourteen months late. The final cost of approximately $900,000 was well over the architects' estimate of $350,000 and the construction bid of $377,978. Financial problems climaxed in mid-1893 with a dispute between the city and contractor John H. Bowman over his failure to pay the bills of subcontractors, for which, by contract, he was completely liable. In July Bowman was fired, and the City Council, by default, took on direct responsibility for the building's construction.[37]

To fend off the mounting bills, the committee issued warrants. Tracy purchased them or accepted them as collateral for loans, later confiding to associates that he made more money in one year from City and County Building warrants than he had at any time since.[38] By applying the capital at his command this way to a critically money-short economy, he also made a significant contribution to one of the more important and long-lasting improvements to the Salt Lake City skyline. Although this particular case was purely business while later efforts were more philanthropic, it was the first of many contributions he would make to the community.

He would continue to invest in such lucrative government paper. In 1896, he was still advertising for "County and state warrants and jury scrip." Nevertheless, mortgages remained the core of the business.

By early 1895, according to the deputy county recorder, there had been "a steady and constant lifting of mortgages" during 1894. "Gradually has he seen the mortgages wiped out; the titles to homes, that had been temporarily overhung by grave dangers restored; and the 'releases' have grown until . . . they had exceeded new mortgages and other encumbering instruments by 50 percent." Since then new mortgages had again begun to accumulate, a sign of increased business for firms like Tracy's but also a sign of greater economic health among the mortgagors. "The additional mortgages meant the release of old ones bearing high rates of interest and the renewal of them at lower, less exacting rates." Property owners were also borrowing to make permanent improvements "to put property in better shape for yielding revenue."[39] By the late 1890s, real estate sales and building construction were once again showing sizable annual increases.

The same newspaper edition which reported the deputy county recorder's statement also listed Russel L. Tracy as a member in good standing of the Salt Lake

Chamber of Commerce. If he had thus achieved one sign of permanence in the community, he was somewhat slower in finding a permanent physical location. By January 1894, he had moved out of Frank Stephens's office and opened his own in the same building: Rooms 41-42, Commercial Block, on the third floor of the old Beeson Building located at 21 East Second South, where a parking terrace for the Walker Bank Building now stands. He probably continued to occupy both rooms, although subsequent directories and advertisements list 42 Commercial Block. A year later, Tracy moved to Room 49 in the same building, expanding into Room 50 by late 1896. Here he stayed until 1899 when he moved out into the Crane Building, 232 South Main Street. In 1902 as a new corporation he opened for business at 11 East First South, across the street from the present headquarters of Tracy-Collins Bank and Trust. This time he did not relocate until he had built a building of his own fourteen years later.[40]

During this period, the company's growth continued to be slow and measured. As late as 1898 Tracy still had only one half-time employee. That year, however, he made a significant addition to his staff with a fourteen-year-old, untried office boy known as Jimmie Collins. Tracy's 1902 decision to incorporate, although it brought him under state regulation, included many advantages. He regularly used special stock subscriptions—not immediately but during subsequent years to raise capital. Perhaps most important to potential clients was the secure image of a corporation. Tracy's reputation may have been excellent among investors, but a corporation with paid-up capital presented unarguable financial strength, much more objective than faith in any one man. Furthermore, any further evolution of the company into more extensive banking virtually required corporate status. The days of private banks were numbered, and they would be prohibited after 1911.[41]

Incorporating as Russel L. Tracy Co. in 1902 were Tracy, his first wife Luella S. Tracy, his ex-roommate Frank B. Stephens, A. N. McIntosh, and W. P. Hemphill. Tracy was elected president and treasurer, Luella Tracy was vice president, and A. N. McIntosh was secretary. The same three constituted the board of directors. The authorized capital stock was $100,000. At $100 per share, Russel Tracy subscribed to 246 shares and the other incorporators one each.

The principal business of the new company was "to transact a general loan, brokerage and commission business." Russel Tracy's method of operation became that of Russel L. Tracy Co.; but the articles of incorporation left the options open, stating that the company's pursuit would be

> . . . to lend money with or without security; to buy and sell, negotiate and assign notes, mortgages, bonds, stocks, and other evidences of indebtedness and securities for the same . . . .
>
> To borrow money by issuing promissory notes, bonds, debentures and certificates of indebtedness, and providing for and securing the payment of same by the deposit, pledge, mortgage, transfer or sale of notes, bonds, mortgages and other securities and real and personal property.

Some activities in which the company was probably already more or less engaged were also stipulated. They were areas into which Tracy would continue to expand in logical extension of his mortgage business:

> To conduct a real estate, rental and insurance agency, to buy, sell and improve real estate.

> . . . to act as trustee under mortgages or deeds of trust, and to act as the assignee and receiver of property and as the executor of wills, and the administrator of estates.[42]

After ten years Russel Tracy was now securely established in Utah. Within the next decade, Tracy began to make major changes, placing more importance on a burgeoning trust operation and planning for a savings department and a new company home. Meanwhile, the real estate market had taken on renewed energy, and the Tracy company was a major beneficiary. In 1906, it made more loans on real estate than any single competitor in Salt Lake City. In 1908 it exceeded its top three rivals; and by 1911, a combination of five could not match the biggest mortgage creditor in the state of Utah.

CHAPTER 3

# Mortgage Broker to Loan and Trust Company, 1902-21

From the beginning Russel Tracy sought to operate his company according to an ethical philosophy that would provide a greater sense of purpose than simply making money. Earning a profit was expected, of course, but employees were encouraged to see their moral responsibility to clients. A set of Tracy's own "Ten Commandments" captured the essence of a philosophical approach which emerged in various company slogans over the years. These commandments emphasized good name and reputation, moral obligation, and protecting clients over financial profits, legal obligation, and business volume. The other things came too, but to Tracy they were secondary. His first motto and commandment was "Not the most but the safest loans."[1] By the early twentieth century, he was making the most as well, an impressive record of growth for a decade and a half. By all indications, he did it without deviating from his own set of priorities. A successor, Newell Dayton, compared

Tracy with J. C. Penney, who had once worked for Dayton's grandfather. Penney had passed up an opportunity to open a business in Ogden, Utah, because he felt unready to take on "such a great metropolis." The two shared the philosophy "that they didn't want to get into something that was too big for them. They wanted to work their way up. That's what Mr. Penney did and that's what Mr. Tracy did with his bank."[2]

Tracy had selected Utah for his business because it offered an opportunity for such steady, slow expansion. The early twentieth century rewarded his foresight. The state's population doubled between 1890 and 1920, and the economy became increasingly monetized and integrated into the national market. The self-sufficient pioneer farmers and artisans, and the free-enterprising miners and merchants began to blend into one secular economy after Utah became a full-fledged member of the national political community. Export-oriented production increasingly dominated agriculture, mining, and manufacturing. Farmers and stockraisers increased their acreage. Dairy, fruit, and sugarbeet industries all received new stimulus. Dry farming and large reclamation projects, beginning with the Strawberry Valley project, opened new areas to agriculture. Mining continued to pursue lower-grade, harder-to-reach ores with new technologies. The growth in copper production was particularly strong, especially after the founding of the Utah Copper Company in 1903. Manufacturing, while experiencing some growth, continued to be a weak part of the state's economy; it was primarily oriented toward first-stage processing of raw materials such as beet sugar and minerals.[3]

All of this activity, especially the greater commercialization and orientation toward national markets, meant sudden growth in the business sector. Retailing, wholesaling, and banking all made impressive strides. Between 1890 and 1910, the number of finance and clerical workers jumped from 1,929 to 7,141 and from 2.9 percent to 5.4 percent of Utah's work force, according to the census. In 1896, there were eleven national and thirty-five private and state banks in Utah. This increased to 28 national and 106 state banks by 1920. Increases were particularly great after 1904. Beginning with fifty-four banks that year, 1905, 1906, and 1913 saw additions with eleven, eleven, and thirteen new operations, respectively. Much of the growth took place outside Salt Lake City and Ogden, as many smaller communities also acquired banking facilities.[4] As early as January 1903, increased dividends from mines, good wheat crops, and an unprecedented year in the beet-sugar industry were reported to be "pouring money into the coffers of banks." Deposits increased nearly $3 million at twelve leading banks during 1902. Loans and discounts did not keep up with this pace, but companies like Tracy could take heart from a "most satisfactory" year in real estate. The panic of 1907 brought a temporary downturn in the first decade's growth, but by the end of 1909, bankers were preparing for unprecedented prosperity after a banner year. They were right; total assets of Utah's banks grew from $44.2 million to $102.6 million between 1910 and 1920.[5]

Tracy, then, benefited from the expanding economy, just as he and other bankers contributed to that growth. But it was not automatic. Fifty-one financial institutions closed between 1896 and 1920. During a panic out of nowhere like that of 1907, businesses like Tracy's were vulnerable in an age before the Federal Deposit Insurance Corporation, or even the Federal Reserve, existed. Tracy's survival and continued growth obviously stemmed from his sound business methods. Before trying anything new, Tracy concentrated on mastering mortgage finance. Clients could appreciate it when, in an age that was producing more specialists to deal with more complex problems, they were told that "years ago, we decided we would not speculate in real estate, purchase mining stocks, invest in commercial paper, or indulge in any form of speculation whatever, but rather devote our entire time, thought and energy to the mortgage loan business, until now we claim we are specialists in this particular line of investments." Tracy insisted that there was no better security than a first lien on other people's homes. It was "not based upon franchises or earnings such as is the case of stocks or corporation bonds."[6]

The Russel L. Tracy Company's record in times of financial crisis was a convincing tribute to the quality of their investments, and Tracy was not shy about pointing this out. In November 1907 he advertised, "During this so-called panic, we have more money than ever to loan on real estate." In 1913 he noted the failure of the First National Bank of Pittsburg for nearly $40 million and that, following the panic of 1893, over one hundred national banks failed for $350 million. He then asked, "Is it any wonder many cautious and observing investors prefer to withdraw their money from the bank . . . and protect it with our first mortgage securities?"[7]

He continued to emphasize this approach during the fall and early winter of 1914. World War I's beginnings in Europe had precipitated a severe crisis in the United States as Europeans converted securities into cash. The New York Stock Exchange was closed from August 1914 to April 1915.

Tracy noted that the consequent depreciation and loss in stocks or securities amounted to more than $500 million and that

> while under present conditions, we may not make much money . . . we expect to continue the unbroken record of the past thirty years, and not only protect every client against loss but repurchase upon request any mortgages we have ever sold. We will thus again prove to our clients . . . as we did in the panics of '93, '94, and '07 that our securities are as quickly converted into cash as any securities in America.

Under the circumstances, *Financial World* agreed that the real estate mortgage was "coming into its own" because it was a "strictly high grade, approved, seasoned security based on the earth and its fullness, the kind that won't turn pale and throw the investor into a fit every time a war extra comes out." Despite such confidence, the Tracy company was not immune. During September, October, and November 1914, more clients asked to sell back their securities than during the previous three years, helping explain the contemporary emphasis on the company's record. Tracy met the demand. During this time, Tracy also had to step up foreclosures and stop increasing the years on his slogan: "Twenty-one years with only one foreclosure." By early 1915, so much money was returning from clients that insufficient loans could be found and the regular circulation of a loan list was delayed three months.[8] When this crisis passed and a war-stimulated boom followed, Tracy could claim an enviable record in dealing with financial hard times.

Loans were carefully selected. Only 20 percent of applications were approved, and the money placed on them represented only 30 to 40 percent of the property's value. Equally important, the company worked hard with mortgagors to help them meet their obligations. Such efforts ranged from giving farmer mortgagors *Better Farming* subscriptions and helping them keep abreast of their changing occupation, to offering to pay tax assessments of mortgagors threatened with public sale.[9] An idea of the type of loans made can be acquired from 1915 loan lists, a year before a move into new headquarters brought changes in the nature and extent of operations. Loans ranged from $125 to $16,000 on properties valued from $400 to $43,500, but 75 percent were for $2,000 or less and half of those were for $1,000 or less. This indicates an emphasis on residences. They were, moreover, city residences; only 9 percent of loans were on farm properties. The average loan had not grown that much from the first three Tracy had made in Cheyenne in the 1880s.[10] The market for them was probably the same as well: young homeowners just getting established, a field Tracy would continue to specialize in.

Meanwhile, Tracy had begun to develop other specialties. The most important was a trust department. In January 1908, the name of Russel L. Tracy Company was changed to Russel L. Tracy Trust Company, and a month later on February 21, became Tracy Loan and Trust Company. This would remain the company name until 1944. It was common for a mortgage lender to end up performing trust functions relative to the real estate and securities it handled. The 1902 articles of incorporation had stated that the company would "act as trustee under mortgages or deeds of trust, . . . as the assignee and receiver of property," and even as an executor of wills and administrator of estates. Such business was not unexpected, but the decision to launch a full-fledged trust operation and to reorient the company by changing its name was a more important step. The lack of strong trust departments in the Salt Lake City area made the move a promising development, and the new department grew rapidly. Eventually it would become the largest operation in the region.[11]

Oddly, the 1908 amendments to the articles, which changed the company name and also reworded the declared pursuit or purpose, did not mention the trust business. This was rectified in 1914 amendments which stated that Tracy Loan and Trust would "act as assignees, agents, receivers, guardians of the estates of minors and incompetent persons, executors and administrators, and . . . execute trusts of every description not inconsistent with law." That year's amendments also contained a provision, removed in later years, that nothing in the articles of Utah statutes "shall be so construed as to authorize or empower this corporation to conduct a bank or engage in the business of banking, and this corporation shall not conduct a bank or engage in the business of banking."[12] Although it was a completely voluntary prohibition, the apparent intent was to make the Bank Commissioner's classification easier.

There was a rather fuzzy line between banks with trust departments and trust companies that performed borderline banking functions like accepting time deposits. The bank examiner since 1903 had been empowered to examine "loan and trust companies, building and loan associations, and insurance companies" as well as banks. The 1911 banking act had rather loosely defined commercial banks as

> any bank authorized by law to receive deposits of money, deal in commercial paper and to make loans thereon, and to lend money on real or personal property, and to discount bills, gold and silver bullion or foreign currency or bulk exchange.[13]

Most of these powers were specifically authorized in Tracy Loan and Trust's articles, so the no-banking provision may have been necessary for clarity.

What happened in 1914 is further confused by the fact that the amended articles seem to have changed Tracy's status with the new independent office of the Bank Commissioner. For the first time, his biannual report listed trust companies as well as banks. While the Tracy Company was included on this list, dated December 1, 1914, it was not included among individual reports to the Commissioner dated November 21, 1914.[14] Tracy's amended articles and a report to the Commissioner were filed on November 30. Apparently Russel Tracy had moved in typically gradual fashion. While he had changed his company's name to include the word trust in 1908, he had specifically disclaimed the requisite powers until 1914 when he felt ready to undertake the new tasks. Until then his business remained essentially loan brokerage and was not subject to the same supervision by the state.

By 1915, Tracy Loan and Trust advertised its services fully. The main business was as estate executors, whereby the company would:

1. Take possession of all property and become familar with the affairs of the estate.
2. List all property in a complete inventory.
3. File returns for payment of Federal and State taxes.
4. Advertise for debts in the manner required by law.
5. Pay legacies and residuary bequests as directed by the will.[15]

The first step, of course, was to get people to make wills declaring the Tracy Company executors. The most elaborate advertising yet employed, nine illustrated pamphlets by Ralph Parlette and distributed by Tracy, explained the advantages of a carefully drawn will. Using clever stories with a moral, these pamphlets discussed the benefits and mechanics of wills, usually with a short statement at the end about the advantages of employing a company rather than an individual as executor. More immediate options were the "Family Estate" or the "Living Trust." With the former, a customer set aside part of his estate for his family's future and the company invested it in securities and insurance. In the Parlette pamphlet a mythical Harry laid it out in capsule form for a friend:

| | |
|---|---|
| My $10,000 of 6% securities | $10,000 |
| $600 yearly Interest, age 35 buys Insurance of | 20,000 |
| Total Family Estate at start | 30,000 |
| Dividends after 5 years increase Estate to | 30,590 |
| After 10 years | 31,265 |
| After 25 years | 33,620 |

A living trust similarly turned a portion of the estate over to the trust company but for a specified time, not necessarily as long as the person's lifetime. He or she then received income from it regularly.[16]

The 1908 amendments had specified that Tracy Loan and Trust would also "conduct a real estate, rental and insurance agency . . . act as Agent for Insurance Companies" and "buy, sell and improve real estate." Furthermore, it would "engage in the business of making and certifying to the correctness of abstracts of title to real estate in any County in the State of Utah."[17] These were all logical spinoffs of mortgage lending. For example, when a loan was made, costs of an abstract, recording, and insurance were deducted from its amount, as shown by a 1914 card-size form.

After 1920, when Tracy bought the Salt Lake

Security and Trust Company's title abstract department, it became important enough for Tracy to keep several men at the courthouse all the time. To justify this expense, publicize the department, and bring in business for other departments, Tracy Loan and Trust offered to use these men to furnish "information for our clients and friends without charge." Real estate men, lawyers, and bankers were told that information "regarding Taxes, Special Assessments, Judgments or other simple information" from the county records would be provided free and without delay.

Newell Dayton, who began his rise to chairman of the Board of Tracy-Collins by service in the abstract department, recalled that his work was not always routine. One day early in the 1920s, he said, he "came back from lunch and there was a fellow having a big fist fight with the manager of the department, who was J. C. Jensen." The man had come in with an abstract "that was all smashed up—it looked terrible." He claimed, "I was getting on the streetcar to come down here with this abstract and the streetcar ran over it, and look what happened." Mr. Jensen refused to swallow this; he "didn't believe you could slip an abstract under a streetcar and have it come out as good as it was." The fist fight resulted. But the fellow soon returned when Jensen was not about. Dayton recalled, "He had timed it so he would come in when everybody was out to lunch. Only I was there; I was at the bottom of the totem pole, so he figured he could take advantage of me where he couldn't those other fellows." Dayton knew though that the man had a bad reputation, so he took the abstract to Mr. Tracy and asked him to pass on it. Tracy backed Dayton up, and there was no further need for fist fights.[18]

Insurance, an integral part of the company's business,

was necessary to secure the real estate backing up the loans. Some of the eastern clients who purchased mortgages were insurance companies. Russel Tracy had been selling insurance as part of his business since his early days in Wyoming, and in 1914 the corporation reiterated the importance by adding the pursuit "to make insurance of every kind pertaining to or connected with titles to real estate" to the existing language in its articles specifying insurance business. Among the companies with which Tracy Loan and Trust did business were National Union Fire Insurance Company, North River Insurance Company, and Hanover Fire Insurance Company.

Business was not limited to insurance associated with real estate such as home and fire. The first automobile arrived in Salt Lake City in 1900. By 1911 there were about two thousand of them in Utah. Within three years of that date, Tracy had sent out a circular which said,

> We have just learned you have recently purchased a new automobile, and we trust you may realize all the pleasure and benefit anticipated.
>
> Many friends will give you suggestions and advice as to what to do in minor trouble with tires, spark plugs, etc., but we venture to offer a suggestion which will fully protect you against the most serious trouble, such as loss or damage of your car by either fire or theft.
>
> If you will sign and mail the enclosed card, our representative will call or communicate with you, and quote rates and explain why we can serve you with automobile insurance better than anyone in the State.

If the introduction of the automobile was the most revolutionary technological change in the pre-World War I period, other social changes also had an impact on Tracy Loan and Trust. The Progressive movement in politics had been responsible for "reform" legislation which sought to improve working conditions and make the workplace a safer and healthier environment. Workmen's compensation, now taken for granted, was one product of this effort. Utah's Workmen's Compensation Act went into effect on July 1, 1917. It required employers with four or more employees to obtain private insurance against accidents to these employees. Tracy had moved quickly to obtain its share of the new business, advertising extensively in the preceding months, offering to inspect work places to help employers reduce risks to their workmen and lower their premiums.[19]

Although it had the power to do so, Tracy Loan and Trust in its early decades generally avoided buying, selling, and holding real estate. Such holdings usually came through foreclosure, and the company prided itself on resorting to such expedients only on the rarest of occasions. In 1916, the first year good records are available, Tracy reported real estate holdings amounting to $49,584. By 1922 this was down to $5,684. The next largest mortgage company in Salt Lake City owned real estate amounting to $393,477. Even much smaller trust companies had larger holdings than Tracy, which had clearly succeeded in avoiding immobilizing resources in this way.[20]

The escrow department wooed contractors:

> In case you sell any of your real estate under contract or on monthly payments, and wish to leave the contract, deed and other papers in escrow for collection, and where they will be perfectly safe and protected against loss by fire, we cordially invite you to consult our escrow department, which is especially equipped for making transfers of property.
>
> We charge nothing for making out the deed, nothing for notary's work, and nothing for any information and suggestions we can give in order to place in proper and legal form the terms of your contract.

Charges were, in 1915, $2.50 upon escrows of $1,000 or less and $5.00 when they were more than $1,000. "For computing interest, making collections and remitting same" a fee of ten cents was charged for each $100 collected. In 1924 Tracy Loan and Trust served as escrow agent during the organization of People's Finance and Thrift, founded with a capital of $100,000 to "loan money to the wage earner, the salaried man and the small tradesman in times of stress, illness, family misfortune, the need of better surroundings, the education of children, the necessity for tools or equipment, all recognized by the company to be legitimate reasons for borrowing."[21]

Between 1902 and 1916 these various activities were conducted out of ground floor offices in the Hooper Building, located at 11 East First South next to the still-standing First Security Building. In the general offices, desks were aligned along one wall of a relatively narrow hall and separated from the walkway by a waist-high partition. One desk, J. W. Collins's, faced outward across this partition, which ended with a curved cashier's cage which jutted further out into the hall. Above the cashier was a mezzanine containing other employees' desks reached by a small staircase at the end of the hall. Tracy had a separate private office at the same location.[22]

As operations expanded, it became wise for Tracy Loan and Trust to increase its capital stock from the original $100,000 authorized in 1902. At a meeting of stockholders on March 26, 1912, the amount went up to $250,000. At the time, Russel Tracy held 897 shares of outstanding stock, James Collins had 100 shares, and Luella Tracy, Frank Stephens, and George Marks, had one share each. Marks was treasurer and secretary of the corporation. The new stock consisted of 500 shares of common stock and 1,000 shares of preferred stock with a par value of $100 each. The preferred stock would have no voting power but would bear a dividend of 5 1/2 percent per annum, paid before any dividend was paid on the common stock. Additional dividends after paying this 5 1/2 percent were divided equally between the preferred and common stock until the former reached 8 percent, after which remaining earnings were applied to the common stock.[23]

Besides raising additional capital, the new stock was offered to clients with the intent "to draw them more closely to us" and reward them for past support with the 8 percent rate, as opposed to the 5 1/2 percent they customarily earned on mortgage securities. The first five hundred shares of preferred stock were offered in 1912 exclusively to clients. In 1914 the other half of the preferred stock was sold, again to clients only and in proportion to the amounts of securities they already held. Tracy preserved the option of repurchasing the shares if the mortgage holdings of the client fell below a certain amount. Tracy assured the clients of the value of the investment, since the company would only need to earn $10,737 to pay the full 8 percent. Moreover, because money could be borrowed at 5 1/2 percent if all the company was interested in was more funds, clients were assured that the primary purpose behind the offer was "to stimulate the interest of our clients in this Company, and also express our appreciation of their valuable patronage."

These sales proved so successful—they were in fact oversubscribed—and resulted in clients bringing increased business to the company—that 100 to 150 of the remaining three hundred shares of common stock were offered to clients in 1915. These had the advantage over preferred stock of not being limited to earnings of 8 percent, although that dividend had to be paid first. Tracy sold the common stock at $600 per share and promised a dividend of $36 a year on each, 6 percent of the investment and 36 percent of their par value. Earnings were expected to be higher than this, but for the present the difference was to be carried to surplus. Josiah Barnett, who had helped Tracy set up in Salt Lake City, was the first purchaser of five shares; District Court Judge C. W. Morse was another early Salt Lake City buyer. Enthusiastic endorsements of the plan also came in from eastern clients. C. C. Wagner of the Wagner Hardware Company in Mansfield, Ohio, wrote,"I would appreciate as many shares as you can see your way clear to allow me, and while I am advised this will be about five shares, if you can double this and make it ten, it will please me proportionately." E. E. Cole, President of National Union Fire Insurance Company, stated that "having knowledge of the achievements of your Company in the past and the high character of its management, promising splendid returns for the future, I am glad to have an opportunity to acquire some of the Common Stock." W. W. Stone of the Hanover Fire Insurance Company said, "I appreciate your remembering me in this matter." And G. W. Blymyer, Jr., of the Blymyer Brothers Company, also in Mansfield, promised "to reciprocate by using any influence I have in increasing your business here." Tracy had thus succeeded in its purpose of involving clients as stockholders and raising capital. Their hopes were met as well, for by 1919 the original 6 percent dividend was increased to 8 percent or $48 per share, which rose to 9 percent in 1920.[24]

The significant growth achieved by Tracy Loan and Trust in the years immediately preceding its expansion into new headquarters can be seen in Table 1 comparing Tracy with other major Salt Lake financial institutions of the time.[25] Although others had a higher volume of loans and discounts as well as deposits (deposits, in the case of Tracy and some of the others, referred to the money received for mortgage securities rather than to savings or checking accounts, neither of which Tracy accepted in 1915), none matched Tracy's growth in either category. An average annual increase of $312,000 or 20 percent in loans and discounts was something the company could rightly point to with pride. With an increase in loans and discounts of almost 60 percent, Tracy Loan and Trust had clearly led the field. Such growth also helps explain why the time had come to find newer, larger, offices.

The facilities and quarters of a financial institution are to some degree a measure of its size and stature. From his start at a single desk in the Commercial Building, Russel Tracy had moved his company through successively larger offices as his business volume had expanded. In 1916, though, he took a bold step that announced his company's autonomy and maturity: the construction of its own building to symbolize the enhanced standing of Tracy Loan and Trust in the Salt Lake financial community. To find a satisfactory design, he first sent a request for building or office photos or floor plans to twenty-eight trust companies and banks around the United States. He then personally visited most major western cities to examine existing buildings. Finally, he hired Walter J. Cooper as architect. In Salt Lake City since 1910, Cooper had participated with others in the erection of the Boston, Newhouse, Newhouse Hotel, Keith-O'Brien, and Walker Bank buildings. Tracy had some definite ideas about what he wanted, and Cooper's design reflects them. The James Stewart Company of

New York, represented by Harry Baum, were building contractors, and Marks and Jones of St. Louis were responsible for interior decoration.[26] The completed building, which still stands at 151 South Main Street, was done in the neo-classical revival style.[27]

Tracy Loan and Trust moved in on August 27, 1916. On the following Monday and Tuesday, August 28 and 29, a public reception was held, in which the "ladies of the St. Mark's Guild assisted . . . by serving light refreshments in the basement." Then it was back to business with two new departments, savings and safety deposit, to run along with the existing loan, abstract, insurance, and trust departments.

The safety deposit vault on the main floor was located next to Tracy Loan and Trust's private vault. Both were designed by the Herring-Hall-Marvin Company of Ohio. Some 26-by-30 feet in size, they were reached through doors weighing thirty thousand pounds, each of which was "so perfectly hung that a child of 4 years can operate it with ease." Inside, the deposit boxes were arranged for easy access. None was closer than two feet to the floor or was out of arm's reach above. Airy passageways went entirely around the vaults to help ventilate the building. The vault was open daily from 8:30 a. m. to 5:30 p. m. and on Saturdays from 8:30 a. m. to 1:00 p. m. and 6:00 to 8:30 p. m. Boxes rented for $1 a year and up in 1916, for $2 and up by 1921. Hours had changed by then as well because of a problem with robberies on Saturday evening when all the employees except two custodians had gone home. On at least one occasion in March 1920 the custodians were locked in the vault after robbers broke into a number of boxes. The Saturday evening shift was subsequently discontinued.[28]

Savings accounts opened at 4 percent interest, and

## Table 1
## LEADING SALT LAKE CITY BANKS, 1912-15

| *Name of Bank* | *Capital* | *Surplus* | *Loans and Discounts* | | *Deposits* | |
|---|---|---|---|---|---|---|
| | | | *1912* | *1915* | *1912* | *1915* |
| National Bank of Republic | $300,000 | $300,000 | $1,767,611 | $2,209,304 | $4,047,602 | $3,561,780 |
| Deseret National Bank | 500,000 | 500,000 | 2,437,715 | 2,425,738 | 3,525,692 | 3,378,513 |
| Continental National Bank | 250,000 | 50,000 | 1,321,552 | 1,559,731 | 2,133,655 | 2,192,843 |
| Utah State National Bank | 600,000 | 120,000 | 2,986,721 | 3,164,944 | 4,452,258 | 3,399,992 |
| National City Bank | 250,000 | 50,000 | | 641,883 | | 997,082 |
| Deseret Savings Bank | 100,000 | 20,000 | 1,432,637 | 1,761,861 | 2,546,495 | 2,740,111 |
| Merchants Bank | 250,000 | | 1,199,090 | 1,133,452 | 1,583,750 | 1,075,973 |
| Walker Brothers | 500,000 | 70,000 | 2,033,233 | 3,219,137 | 3,251,628 | 4,528,186 |

| | | | | | | |
|---|---|---|---|---|---|---|
| Salt Lake Security &Trust Company | 300,000 | | 1,580,492 | 1,622,524 | 1,921,141 | 2,128,272 |
| Farmers & Stock-growers Bank | 300,000 | 12,000 | | 392,894 | | 412,834 |
| Utah Savings & Trust Co. | 300,000 | 30,000 | 761,071 | 821,335 | 1,213,698 | 1,117,749 |
| Zion's Savings Bank & Trust Co. | 500,000 | 250,000 | 4,721,320 | 5,051,196 | 5,701,405 | 6,509,021 |
| McCornick & Company | 600,000 | 120,000 | 3,790,583 | 4,319,570 | 7,005,698 | 6,549,928 |
| Tracy Loan & Trust Co. | 117,500 | 45,404 | 1,575,893 | 2,513,226 | 1,470,135 | 2,322,484 |

*Source:* "Bank Statements" Scrapbook in Tracy-Collins Scrapbooks, Salt Lake City, Utah.

the company used a variety of techniques to market them with a fairly predictable emphasis on the virtues of thrift among old and young. Gifts such as home banks were offered. At one point Tracy opened free accounts containing a nominal initial deposit for a select list of potential customers. Those who had already deposited were offered free tours of the bank and encouraged to use other departments. They were told that when their account reached a few hundred dollars it could be converted into a mortgage security, netting 5 1/2 percent interest. On the other side of the coin, clients were encouraged to deposit their mortgage interest in a savings account. When this amount reached $300, they too could purchase a new mortgage at the higher interest.

Another indication of Tracy's growth during these years was its steady acquisition of new employees. In 1914 there were fifteen men (it was not yet customary to employ women in banks) working for the company. By January 1915 this increased to eighteen; six months later there were twenty-two; and by early 1916, twenty-six. When the new building opened, the Tracy Loan and Trust workforce had doubled in two years, reaching thirty.

The most important positions in the company were the officers authorized by the articles of incorporation. Russel Tracy was, of course, president. His vice-president for many years, James W. Collins, was destined to play an ever more important role in company affairs. The position of secretary and treasurer varied more frequently. By 1908, W. P. Hemphill had replaced A. N. McIntosh. From at least 1912 through the war years, George E. Marks held this job. His assistant was W. R. Granville who became treasurer in 1918 (Marks remained secretary) before moving to the position of secretary of the new Central Trust Company when it opened in 1922. By 1919 N. C.

Ellis was secretary at Tracy, a position he held for several subsequent years. Department heads were highly visible; the company was particularly proud, for example, when in 1918 it secured the services of E. W. Genter as trust officer because he had previously worked as manager of Utah Saving and Trust and was already known in the community. Previous trust officers had been C. Judd Evans and H. L. Selley. Selley returned when Genter did not work out and took on the additional tasks of treasurer when Granville departed. Besides its Salt Lake City employees, the company from time to time maintained representatives in other areas. In 1916 and 1917 W. H. Ray was representative for Utah County loans and the firm of Bothwell and Swaner for Weber County.

The ethical sensitivity Russel Tracy had for his clients was fully reflected with his staff as well. He voluntarily increased salaries every year. From the employees' perspective, one of the more pleasant annual events was the distribution of cash New Year's presents, later Christmas bonuses. In a day when the average employees' annual salary was considerably less than $2,000, the gift in 1914—more than $6,200—must have been especially gratifying. Divided among the eighteen staff members, it came to more than $340 apiece. One of the then more novel techniques used "to make work workable" was an employees' lunchroom added in 1920. The *Salt Lake Herald* considered this step progressive enough to feature it in an article. By that time women also worked at Tracy Loan and Trust, but progress on some related social issues was still evolving. The *Herald* reported that in the electric grille-equipped room, "men employees of the company, not gifted with culinary talent, have managed to achieve the desired end by collective bargaining with the young women employees of the company, who don't mind cooking, but who do hate washing dinner dishes."[29]

At the time Tracy Loan and Trust moved into its new offices, the international situation was deteriorating. When war in Europe first erupted in 1914, the company, apparently reflecting its leading officer's own repugnance at the violence, went so far as to advertise:

> You may question the wisdom and find little satisfaction in investing money in bonds yielding 5 1/2% when you know your money will be used to produce bloodshed, widows and orphans, but it is a great satisfaction to make an investment at the same rate when you know your money is used to assist a father to buy or build a home for himself and his happy family.

When 1917 brought the United States into the conflict, though, Tracy Loan and Trust was offering to "receive subscriptions for United States Liberty Loan Bonds paying 3 1/2 percent, without profit to ourselves."[30]

In the years before American involvement, as the European war stimulated the United States and Utah economies, the Tracy company had no trouble attracting investment, but mortgages to back this investment were becoming scarce. Tracy had difficulty finding sufficient satisfactory mortgages to keep its own funds profitably occupied, let alone those of its clients. The needs of financing the war then brought new problems in linking mortgagors with investors. During 1918, Tracy avoided any impression that he might wish to compete with the government for funds needed for the war effort by not releasing a loan list. Only after subscriptions for the fourth Liberty Loan had closed was such a list again mailed out.

A new technique to attract business from clients was begun in 1919. Instead of just offering single mortgages for sale, large loans on business properties were sold in "First Mortgage Participating Notes." These were offered in denominations of $500 and $1000, and the client shared the mortgage with others.

To attract more customers, Tracy emphasized that it was willing to renew loans at maturity and did not require monthly payments on the principal as long as interest was kept paid. Monthly payments were becoming a more common method of payment because of the difficulty borrowers often faced in paying off a loan all at once. But Tracy was bucking the tide by counting on those who found a monthly schedule difficult. An option for yearly payment on the principal was available, but the company focused on assuring potential customers, such as those who had borrowed from a building society, that they could keep money from Tracy for "as long as they can use it to advantage."

Despite such problems, Tracy Loan and Trust kept up a steady pace of growth during most of the war years. Between February 1915 and March 1918, loans and discounts increased by $522,834.

That same year the company took a symbolic but major step in the evolution of its corporate identity. The paragraph in the articles which had prohibited Tracy Loan and Trust from conducting a banking business was eliminated. Operations did not change. The move was made primarily to catch up with the changed status that opening a savings department in 1916 had brought. But it indicated a change in self-image and future direction. Russel Tracy explained in a letter to stockholders that the company expected "to conduct more of the business of a Savings Bank" and consequently wished to remove the self-imposed limitation. Other Salt Lake City firms were moving in a similar direction. Of those doing business in

1919 with the word *trust* in their titles, two—Zion's Savings Bank and Trust and Utah Savings and Trust—were already classified as banks by the state bank commissioner. Another, Halloran-Judge Loan and Trust, was the basis of what many years later would become First Security State Bank. Salt Lake Security and Trust Company closed in 1920. Only Bankers Trust Company retained that status, merging in 1931 with Central Trust to form First Security Trust Company. Its continued existence as a trust company in fact forced a separation of First Security's nonbanking assets in 1959, when the differences between banks and other financial institutions were more clearly defined.[31]

Tracy, then, was not alone in its evolution toward being more clearly a bank. Looking back in 1919, however, few financial concerns of whatever type could point out such phenomenal change as the company which in 1892 had come to Salt Lake City as a one-man mortgage brokerage. More changes would come, though, and it would still be several decades before Tracy was a complete commercial bank.

Another step in this direction came in 1919 when Tracy joined the Federal Reserve System. Authorized in 1913, the Federal Reserve became operative in 1914. Twelve regional banks were organized; member banks' reserves were centralized; capitalization requirements and examination procedures were tightened; and other regulations were changed with the primary object of establishing a central banking system. National banks were required to join, but state banks were free to choose. In Utah they chose not to join until World War I brought patriotic pressure on them to do so. In 1918 the first Utah banks took the step. For Tracy, joining meant changing some procedures, but more importantly it meant new ammunition in conveying the image of safety and conservatism which the company was already selling: "We have always been able and willing to cash upon request any securities we have ever sold. How much more attractive should these loans prove hereafter, since, in an emergency, we can call upon the Federal Reserve Bank for assistance in order to protect the interests of our clients."[32] Ironically, the Federal Reserve's erratic monetary policies soon contributed to postwar problems in Utah's economy.

The decade between 1910 and 1920 had been one of the most prosperous for Utahns. Annual per capita income grew from $183 to $556. Manufacturing, agriculture, transportation, and mining led growth in all areas. Moreover, working conditions improved due to high wages, safer workplaces, better hours and laws regulating the employment of women and children. The climax of these better days came during World War I as demand for Utah products, primarily foodstuffs and metals, boomed.[33]

The inevitable contraction after the war culminated with the national depression of 1921 which was symbolized by the sudden collapse of commodity prices. The severest blow fell on isolated states like Utah whose growth had been tied to the previous inflated prices and who now could not compete in contracted markets. The immediate postwar years of 1919 to 1922 were the worst period for the state, but Utah did not really recover until after the depression of the 1930s.

Banking struggled as well as other areas of the economy. Problems began in 1919 with a precipitous rise in the discount rate for prime commercial paper. The Federal Reserve was not much help to an increasingly money-short Utah economy. As one scholar of the subject observed:

The Federal Reserve Board was so concerned with financing federal debt operations that it allowed the discount rate to remain at 4 3/4 percent until January 1920, when it announced an abrupt increase to 6 percent. This policy of loose money followed by stringent contraction probably contributed to the increase in the prime commercial rate of Salt Lake City's banks from 6 percent to 7 percent and to the continuing increase during 1920, while Utah's economy plummeted from its peak prosperity.[34]

The years between 1921 and 1933 were marked by numerous bank failures, beginning in 1920 when eight banks closed. In 1921 seven more went under; in 1922, thirteen. At a slower rate, closings continued to outpace new bank openings through the 1920s, climaxing in the first years of the 1930s with Utah's worst period of failures. The problems were greatest for small banks in small towns. They had shown a phenomenal increase in numbers in preceding years, and with the collapse of commodity prices, banks dependent on farm business found it difficult to collect on loans.

The larger banks continued to grow during the 1920s, but most of them too had to weather the problems of the early years of the decade. The worst year for Tracy Loan and Trust was 1920, a year when all of Salt Lake City's larger banks lost business—as measured by loans and discounts—except Utah State National Bank and Deseret Savings Bank. Both of them also fell off the next year. Tracy in February 1920 had loans and discounts amounting to $3,610,122, which dropped $3,569,852 a year later. This was hardly a precipitous decline; and within another year the lost ground had been recovered and more. From then, throughout the decade, Tracy, in defiance of general conditions, showed phenomenal growth at a rate matched only by Walker Brothers, whose rise had been stimulated by their takeover of McCornick and Company in 1921.[35] In 1922 Tracy recorded 1,073 mortgages at the Salt Lake County Recorder's office, while its nearest competitor recorded 318. That same year it "received $722,620 new money in addition to what was returned for the purchase of our securities." On a more personal level, Russel Tracy could point out, as evidence of continuing loyalty, that one of his 1,923 clients was the great-grandchild of one of the investors who had helped start him out in 1884. In 1926 it passed Zion's Savings Bank and Trust Company to become Utah's second largest bank after Walker Brothers.[36]

Perhaps Tracy's success can in part be attributed to a willingness to engage its times. In communicating to clients, it did not deny that times were bad—it merely pointed out that "as we note the unsettled condition of stocks and bonds and the depreciation of almost all forms of investment . . . there is no better investment to be found between the Atlantic and the Pacific than the mortgages purchased from us." Bold words, but apparently their clients agreed. The company used other current events in their marketing as well. In 1920 they claimed that mortgages were "the one form of investment which is not affected by politics . . . regardless of whether Harding or Cox wins." For most Americans, the 1920s were the climax of a long period of industrialization and modernization; they were ready to take advantage of the many new things available to them. Tracy offered home improvement loans to people wishing to add such "modern conveniences" as "a furnace, sleeping porch, hardwood floors, bath, and hot and cold water."

And Russel Tracy was ready to demonstrate his own loyalty to Salt Lake City. He advertised its advantages along with his company's, regularly sending out a lavishly illustrated brochure prepared by the Commercial

Club and the Chamber of Commerce, "Salt Lake City: The Center of Scenic America." Business circulars pointed out any signs of upturn in the city's industrial and business conditions. And, now in his sixties, Tracy's scrupulous sensitivity to ethical considerations led him in the direction of philanthropy.

Russel Lord Tracy, the Hunter, 1881.
Shown with his 45-90 Marlin Rifle.

Salt Lake City Main Street as it looked about the time Russel Tracy arrived in 1892

Tracy (on right) instructing newsboys in art of camping and cooking "Mulligan Stew"

Tracy with Newsboys at Thanksgiving Dinner, 1912

Tracy receiving Newsboys with Report Cards, 1922

Tracy With Waterfowl

Tracy Aviary: Tracy With Rare Birds

Tracy Wigwam in Mill Creek Canyon, Salt Lake Valley

Friendship Wall, with Tracy and Katie

Typical Tracy Ads in 1920s

CHAPTER 4

# Tracy-Style Transition, 1921-33

Tracy Loan and Trust experienced an unmatched pace of growth in the 1920s. Loans and discounts almost quadrupled between 1921 and 1931, outdistancing the rate of growth of all other Salt Lake City banks. Tracy emerged as a top power in the Salt Lake City financial community just in time for the Great Depression. Tracy Loan and Trust was not hurt as soon or as severely as other Utah financial houses, but its significant drop in business coincided with changing management. With extraordinary continuity, the bank continued to reflect the personal vision of founder and principal owner Russel Tracy while James Collins and other officers took on greater responsibility for actual operations.

By the 1930s, Tracy had become one of Salt Lake City's best-known and most-loved philanthropists. His "hobbies" were becoming the benefactor and best friend of the city's street newsboys and, then, through the Tracy Aviary and Tracy Wigwam, a Scout campground, the patron of all local children. While, strictly speaking, these were personal activities, they brought recognition to the bank, enhanced its reputation for responsible citizenship, and reflected Russel Tracy's efforts to return to the community some of the success it had given his business. Moreover, attitudes with which he ran his private philanthropies and his bank harmonized markedly.

Russel Tracy had an abiding interest in the success of youth, perhaps because of the loss of his own two sons. Edward died in infancy, and Russel, Jr., died in his twenties. Tracy's interest in the welfare of the city's youngsters, however, had preceded these tragedies, beginning with the personal interest he took in his employees, often referring to them as his "family." Many of them joined at a quite young age; even college graduates started at the bottom as errand boys. The two men who succeeded Tracy as chairman of the board had each apprenticed for a year as errand boys. Each employee—as long as he or she met the criteria of honest, hard work—gradually rose through the ranks, learning a little about every aspect of the business by working in every department. One employee recalls moving from messenger boy to checking vacant houses for the property management department, to loan collections, to teller in the loan division, to savings department teller, to appraiser for mortgage loans, to making up the paperwork for mortgage loans, to broker in the bank's realty company:

> Mr. Tracy changed the people from job to job so that everybody in the bank knew everybody else's job, and it finally ended up that I had worked in every department except the trust department. He returned one year from his winter trip to California or Arizona. He walked in the front door and he walked down the line, and he said,

> "What, you're still here?" I was a teller in the savings cage, and my heart leaped. Had he asked that I be fired or what? I said "Yes sir, I'm still here." Well about ten minutes later I was over in another department. He just didn't want me in the department he had left me in when I could be learning something else.[1]

One important benefit was in customer service. Any employee who was overloaded with customers could call upon anyone else for help.

Longevity with the company rewarded loyalty. Everyone felt reasonably secure of a job, had some kind of personal relationship with the boss, and benefited directly in the company's success through its annual bonuses, a complex form of profit-sharing that compensated seniority. After payment of the regular dividend, one-half of net annual profits were distributed among the officers and employees; 25 percent was distributed in proportion to the length of the time the employee had worked for the company; a second 25 percent was in proportion to yearly salaries; and the remaining 50 percent recognized unusual, special, or meritorious service. At the end of 1927, $10,000 was passed out; in 1928 forty employees divided $10,416; in 1929 forty-seven received $12,347; but by the end of 1930 the Depression was causing adjustments that reduced the bonus to $8,000.[2]

Perhaps the most well-received employee benefit—one which Tracy classified among his "hobbies"—was the Tracy Club on Henry's Fork of the Snake River at Macks Inn near Yellowstone National Park. Since his journeys in the 1880s with General Sheridan and the founding investors in his company, Russel Tracy had regularly returned to Yellowstone and the Snake River. He had taken his namesake son, Russel, Jr., on horseback in 1910 for the entire round trip between Salt Lake City and Henry's Fork. They had camped and fished near the spot where the Tracy Club was built. In 1936 the Forest Service agreed to lease the site. The clubhouse was built in 1937. A large, two-story cabin contained eight spacious bedrooms with double bunk beds. A permanent caretaker did the cooking in a detached dining room. Tracy had his own cabin nearby where he continued to spend annual fishing vacations. The only requirement for employees was to pay for their trip and bring along a towel and soap. Once there, all further expenses of a week's stay with their whole family or a guest couple were paid. The Club still operates on the same basis, although time-of-stay and guest privileges have been reduced because of the much greater number of employees today.[3]

Despite the generosity of his Tracy Club, Tracy was not a "soft" taskmaster. While he offered his staff many incentives, he expected old-fashioned work habits. On one occasion, an employee vacationing with family was summoned to the boss's cabin to take down some letters. The staff member demurred; he did not know shorthand. He could take them in longhand then. The employee did, then was provided with a typewriter. With visions of his vacation slipping away, the employee had a stroke of luck—help from his wife, a more seasoned typist.[4]

Tracy's philanthropy sometimes included his less fortunate customers. It was not uncommon for him to pay the taxes of a widow who was threatened with the loss of her home to the county. Occasionally, according to Newell Dayton, he would even help widows by buying back properties sold for taxes:

> Here you would have a home and the husband had been a little short on judgment when he built it and had never paid for it. The husband died and left a wife with a

> number of children and no way of taking care of it. Mr. Tracy would buy up those tax sales and he would carry them along.... then at some proper time he would go to the widow and have a kind of seance with her as to where she stood. She may have been out mopping floors or sweeping an office; she was making her way by sheer hard work. And yet she was teaching her children to live frugally and to grow, and he was impressed with that family. So he would gather the family together and tell them how important thrift was and so forth.
>
> I was with him once. This wasn't a big home that this lady had, and she had seven or eight children and she was having a rough time getting along. But he had watched her—he would take quite a little interest in finding out how worthy these people were—and he gave this oration about how you should take care of your obligation, and he was quite critical of the husband who had left his lady without any wherewithal. When he got through he reached in his pocket, brought out a deed to the property all cleared—nothing owing on it at all. He said, "I'm giving you this as a token of my real feeling. I'm just not talking about something that I don't really believe in." After he got through, he said to me, "I get more pleasure out of doing something for somebody else than any so-called pleasures that I could go out and buy for my own, just because it is something I would like."[5]

To pre-1930s residents of Salt Lake City, Russel Tracy was best-known as "the newsboys' best friend." For almost forty years on Thanksgiving, the city's young street news vendors could be seen and heard marching from Deseret Gymnasium where Tracy had assembled them to some restaurant or hall where dinner with all the trimmings was served, followed by a movie. They carried banners proclaiming their gratitude and accomplishments and cheered or chanted such ditties as this 1917 composition by "Micky":

Who are we?
Who are we?
Guests of the Tracy com-pan-ee!
We're hot stuff,
That's no bluff,
We eat turk
And can't get 'nough!

This annual tradition of dinner and recreation had begun in 1902 when Tracy became acquainted with an impoverished youth named Ralph Nielson.[6] That year, he provided Ralph's family with Thanksgiving dinner, and the following year he and Ralph hosted all of the youngster's fellow newsboys. The city's newspapers cooperated; Charlie McGillis, the *Telegram*'s street circulation manager, coordinated events. Utah's governor and the city's mayor or chief of police always attended. Beginning in 1913, the boys also got warm stockings and shoes.

Tracy did not limit his interest to a once-a-year event. He visited and helped their families; he furnished transportation for excursions to Yellowstone and Jackson Hole, Wyoming. He took them on week-long camping trips in the Cottonwood Canyons, and he equipped a downtown gymnasium for them. Perhaps most important was the year-long advice and encouragement he offered them on schoolwork, thrift, and personal habits. He rewarded academic efforts by personally examining report cards, offering fifty cents for each "excellent," twenty-five cents for "very good," and ten cents for "good." At the end of the year, the newsboy with the best overall record received a new suit of clothes. Many of these newsboys, ranging from heavyweight boxer Jack Dempsey to Secretary of State Clyde Miller, went on to successful careers. But Tracy was proudest of Utah Governor Herbert B. Maw, who freely acknowledged the influence of "the newsboys' godfather" in his inaugural address in 1941. "Mr. Tracy," said the new governor, "has been an inspiration to me, and I value highly the precepts of honesty and industry which he taught me." Later, publishing his autobiography on the occasion of his ninetieth birthday, Maw recalled Tracy's practice of paying newsboys for their report cards:

> It must have been a strange sight for customers of the bank to see a line of newboys heading for his bank every report day to receive a reward for diligence. That recognition, given to us by a successful man, motivated many of us for good. I was happy to be able to let the citizens of this state learn of his inspiration to me, as a youngster, by inviting him to sit on the stand when I was inaugurated Governor of Utah and by publicly revealing his tremendous contribution to my life, years before.[7]

Tracy's help to the street vendors ended in 1941 when new laws restricted the job to young men over sixteen.

Outside of his bank, Tracy's name has been preserved in two Salt Lake area institutions, Tracy Wigwam in Mill Creek Canyon and Tracy Aviary in Liberty Park. He had taken an active interest in the Boy Scouts of America since their founding, supporting a variety of outdoor activities. In 1921 he built Tracy Wigwam campground as a memorial to his two sons and donated it to the Boy Scouts. Tracy Aviary grew out of a private bird collection which Mr. and Mrs. Tracy had assembled and displayed in their extensive yard at 1285 Second Avenue. As the collection became popular among visitors, the Tracys conceived the idea of donating it to the city and placing it in Liberty Park for the benefit of the children. Tracy saw this as a way to show his love of Salt Lake City and "to express my appreciation to those who have contributed to my success, and to the early pioneers and settlers whose courage, trials, hardships, and suffering transformed this barren sagebrush country into a beautiful and promising valley." The gift included 200 birds and other animals and $10,000 for further purchases. The Tracy Aviary Commission which set up shop in April 1938 was headed by James W. Collins who continued to serve the Tracy Aviary long after Russel Tracy's death.[8]

Collins's involvement in one of Tracy's most important philanthropies was not unusual. Although many young men, in and out of the bank, could say that Tracy had been like a father to them, no one could say it with the same truthfulness as James Collins. Collins had been born in Cheyenne on June 1, 1884, the year and place that Tracy founded his company, to William E. and Anna Louise Henderson Collins. They had been acquainted with Russel Tracy in Cheyenne, a fact that had an enormous influence on their son's life. They moved to Salt Lake City in 1894 when James was ten. After a few years attending public schools in the city, James approached Tracy for a summer job. Tracy retells the meeting with relish in his autobiography:

> In June, 1898, a little undersized, rosy-cheeked boy of fourteen in knee pants, entered one of the modest business houses, handling mortgage loans, of Salt Lake City, addressing the president: "Mister, have you any work I could do to keep me off the streets during the summer vacations?"
>
> The president knew he had no place for the boy, but wished to give him a lesson which in later years he might use to advantage and be prepared to answer questions in applying for a position. Therefore, he asked the boy if he used cigarettes or tobacco, how he got along in school deportment and scholarship, what he did to help his mother, if he brought in the kindling and started the fires,

etc. So pleased was he with the boy's replies that he became embarrassed because he had nothing to offer him (as he found it difficult to pay the salary of his own employee who worked for him but one-half of each day). He gave the boy the names of several prominent firms whom he suggested the boy call upon and later return and report the results of the visits.

A few days later the boy returned, saying he had called upon all of the firms the president [Tracy] had mentioned but was unsuccessful in finding employment. Again he was given names of other prominent firms with whom the president thought it was possible the boy could find employment.

Again the boy returned and while standing on one foot with legs crossed said, "I guess they don't like me; they all tell me I am too little or that they have no use for a boy." The result was that the president said they would have to make a place for the boy, and he was engaged as the second employee at $2 a week or $8 a month for the summer.

A few weeks later the president met with an accident and was totally blind for more than a month, during which period the boy was accustomed to lead him to and from his home. By September he had endeared himself to his employer who saw rare possibilities in the boy. Consequently, I called upon the boy's mother and also the superintendent of public schools and suggested that unless they had other plans and brighter prospects, I would suggest that the boy continue his studies at night school and come into my office in the daytime that he might be trained for a position there.

At the time I little thought that forty-three years later, as I reviewed the past, this little boy of fourteen years would greatly contribute to my happiness and success; that he would succeed me as President of the Tracy Loan & Trust Company; that he would contribute to all of my hobbies including the newsboys, Boy Scouts, and Mt. Olivet Cemetery Association; and that without him there would be no Tracy Aviary or Tracy Club. In fact, he has

> for forty-three years shared my every joy and sorrow so that with the exception of my wife there is no one to whom I owe so much or love so much as James or "Jimmie Collins."[9]

By the time in 1933 that James Collins assumed the presidency of Tracy Loan and Trust, he had already achieved considerable standing of his own in the community. In becoming vice president of Tracy Loan and Trust in 1907 at the age of twenty-two, he served as chairman of Utah's World War I savings bond drive at age thirty-three, became president of the Salt Lake City Rotary Club at thirty-five, and was president of the Salt Lake Country Club at forty. He held numerous positions in local fraternal organizations at a young age. Such community activity and service continued in later years when he headed organizations as diverse as the Mortgage Bankers Association of America; the Victory Loan, War Chest, Red Cross, and Community Chest Campaigns Committees during World War II; Salt Lake City Chamber of Commerce; and the Mount Olivet Cemetery Association. He directed the construction of the Meditation Chapel in Memory Grove and helped devise and run a campaign to finance construction of Salt Lake City's Masonic Temple. While participating in the advancement of Russel Tracy's charitable interests, Collins developed his own, many of which he insisted on keeping secret. Blaine Simons, who at times delivered gifts of suits, checks, and cash for Collins, was told that no one except they and the recipients were to know about it.[10]

By taking over as president in 1933, Collins was responsible for guiding the bank through the toughest period of its history; but previous to that, while still vice president of Tracy Loan, he had also shared the responsibility for the company's fullest realization of Russel

Tracy's early dreams. During the 1920s the bank grew at a phenomenal rate, adding an average of almost $1 million in loans and discounts each year. The best year was between October 1925 and October 1926 when loans and discounts increased by $1.3 million. But as the following list shows, all years were good.

| Year (as of October) | Loans and Discounts |
|---|---|
| 1921 | $3.6 million |
| 1922 | 4.0 |
| 1923 | 4.7 |
| 1924 | 5.5 |
| 1925 | 6.5 |
| 1926 | 7.8 |
| 1927 | 9.0 |
| 1928 | 10.1 |
| 1929 | 11.1 |

On the eve of the stock market crash, Tracy Loan and Trust Company had loans and discounts of $11,184,872. Total resources had grown from $4,321,126 in 1922 to $11,693,564 in 1929. During roughly the same period the increase in resources for all state banks in Utah was from $88.1 million to $136.2 million, an average annual increase of 8 percent. Tracy's average annual increase in resources was 24 percent. On the other side of the ledger, time deposits, including trust funds, time certificates, and savings deposits had grown from $488,439 to $884,388 between 1922 and 1929.[11]

The loan lists sent to clients reflected the increased credit activity. The lists were longer, mailed out every two months instead of every three months, and included more large loans. Despite the sluggishness of agriculture and mining, new building construction boomed locally during the 1920s. Demand for both residential and commercial buildings was high, and loans from the Tracy bank helped make them available. Large sums were loaned on apartment houses and business properties and sold in participating notes of $500 and $1000, though most mortgages for commercial buildings were still high, and loans from the Tracy Bank helped make them available. Most mortgages were still for single-family city residences. During several years in the early 1920s when the farm economy remained depressed, no farm mortgages were even listed. As a typical property in 1926, the bank described a new residence in the southeast area of the city. It stood on a 40 x 125 foot lot valued at $800 and was a five-room, "strictly modern," brick dwelling with a cement basement, hot air heating, and hardwood floors. It was insured for $2,600 and valued at $4,700. The total valuation of house and lot was thus $5,500. The loan was for $2,500, roughly 45 percent of the value.

Tracy Loan and Trust's methods continued much the same. Loans represented 40 to 50 percent of a property's value. Improvements were insured for at least the amount of the loan. Interest for over twenty years remained at 6 percent, of which the client netted 5 1/2 percent. The term of the loan was usually three, but sometimes up to five years. Each loan had to have the written approval of two bank officers who had personally examined the property; the approval of three officers was required for loans of more than $5,000. Mortgages were not guaranteed, but the title to the property and the fact that the mortgage was a first lien on it were. In case of trouble with the mortgage, such as failure to keep up the property, the bank repurchased the mortgage and absorbed any losses.

Russel Tracy's careful, conservative approach was

the basis of his success. He was legendary for insisting that his employees pick up paper clips on the floor and turn out restroom lights when not in use, but the same methods which applied to larger questions were equally legendary. By 1927, investors in Tracy's mortgages lived in Canada, England, Ireland, China, South America, Mexico, Hawaii, the Philippines, and twenty-seven different states. A growing number of them lived in Utah as well.

The safe, conservative record of Tracy's mortgage business was used to sell the company's other services. Potential clients of the trust department, for example, might be particularly interested in a statement such as, "There is not an officer, director or employee indebted to this Company for a single dollar loaned them, or upon any paper endorsed by them." The Tracy company had benefited from getting in early on the still young trust company business, which by 1928 amounted to some $21 billion nationally. Trust funds were still a relatively small portion of the company's overall business, but they were profitable. The fees mandated by laws were 5 percent on the first $1,000 of an estate, 3 percent on the next $9,000, 2 percent on the next $10,000, and 1 percent on everything over $20,000.[12]

The savings department concentrated on recruiting small accounts—only $1.00—to encourage the habit of thrift. The insurance department sold every type of insurance except life insurance and, by the early 1930s, was the general or local agent for Ocean Accident and Guaranty Corporation, National Union Fire Insurance Company, Hartford Fire Insurance Company, Commercial Union Assurance Company, Insurance Company of North America, Great American Insurance Company, and American Surety Company. In the mid-1920s, the property management department oversaw properties acquired through foreclosure and managed apartment houses for other owners.

Officers of the bank remained mostly the same through the 1920s. Besides Tracy and Collins, Harvey L. Selley was still treasurer and N. C. Ellis continued as secretary. William V. Rockefeller was trust officer until 1930 when Selley once again added those duties to his assignment. An important addition was Newell B. Dayton who, typically, joined the firm as errand boy in 1922 and by 1927 had risen to assistant treasurer. By early 1932 he graduated to treasurer; W. S. Emms took over the other half of Selley's duties as trust officer. Another quickly rising employee was Russel Tracy's nephew Rufus A. Tracy, Jr., who moved from manager of the property management department to assistant treasurer in 1932 and treasurer in 1933. Other long-term officers were Auditor A. B. Davis (succeeded by W. E. Shurtleff in 1932), manager of the insurance department E. Hugh Miller, and savings department manager J. L. Preece. The board of directors increased from three to seven members in 1915 and from seven to nine in 1930. Almost half were bank officers—but some of the longest serving members were Attorney Frank Stephens; Leon Sweet, president of Sweet Candy Company; and C. B. Hawley, general manager of Inter-Mountain Electric Company. Louis Marcus, prominent capitalist and mayor of Salt Lake City, also served for a number of years before his death in 1936.

The officers' community standing was undoubtedly helpful in bringing the company business. For example, both Russel Tracy and James Collins were active Masons. In addition to many useful business contacts, Collins developed a financing plan for the Masonic Temple, constructed in 1929, whereby contributors bought $100 Masonic Temple Notes and came into the bank to make monthly $5 payments on them. Although the bank provided this service without cost, it brought potential customers into the bank. One observer compared it to the contemporary practice of newstands which also provided a laundry service. Like men who brought along their shirts when they came to get their paper, individuals who came to make payments might, after examining the bank, decide to open a savings account. Tracy had long employed such "cross-selling" techniques, offering mortgage securities to savings depositors and vice-versa, for example.[13]

To attract client investors Tracy increasingly emphasized one aspect of its record during the 1920s. That was the convertibility of its securities. Without promising or guaranteeing to do so, the bank had consistently followed the practice "to cash or repurchase immediately upon request, any security or mortgage we have ever sold, without discount or loss to any client of a dollar of principal, or interest due, and regardless of date of maturity." Faced with such a history of almost risk-free investment, it is no wonder that clients were helping Tracy Loan and Trust achieve unprecedented growth. The *Coast Banker* took note of this "impressive statement," including the company's record of meeting repurchase requests within twenty-four hours.[14]

After the stock market crash in 1929, Tracy's record looked particularly impressive to many investors who observed the fate of other securities. But the bank had for years openly compared its mortgage investments with the stock market. As early as January 1925, Russel Tracy pointedly informed investors, "If you wish to speculate and enjoy the thrill and excitement of an advance in the market, also the worry and anxiety of a depressing one, others can serve you better than we, as we never speculate either for ourselves or others." When the New York Stock Exchange had its worst month yet in March 1926, the bank pointed out to clients that the drop in value of securities had been between $5 million and $10 million while Tracy's mortgage securities had never dropped even $1 in value. Then after the October 1929 crash, Tracy publicists rubbed it in: "Where is your money? Invested in safe, dependable securities, or in those subject to the fluctuation of a rapidly changing market?"[15]

There was perhaps a little gloating here based on depressions and panics of the past. Tracy Loan and Trust would soon learn that no one would escape the Great Depression, although there was a considerable lag between the onset of hard times (symbolized, though not caused by, the stock market crash) and any serious drop in the bank's business. Outwardly, "business as usual" was maintained well into 1931. Confident comparisons between mortgage securities and the stock market were part of the company's marketing strategy until early 1932. By then, mortgage investments also faced serious problems. Despite the confident face turned to the public—an absolutely necessary psychological tool in banking—Tracy had not been unconcerned. Almost simultaneously with the crash, the company had mobilized its efforts to manage the approaching crisis.

The causes of the Great Depression are still debated by economists and historians. It is clear, however, that some of the disaster's roots must be found in the prosperity of the Twenties. After the disillusioning brutality of modern industrial warfare, Americans had turned away from World War I to enjoy the more pleasant peacetime products of industry, which they felt they had earned. Automobiles, bathtubs, electric appliances, and radios were among the new products available in mass quantities. Advertising came of age in the 1920s as consumers heard pitch after pitch for each new symbol of the new prosperity, now easy to get with installment buying.

Despite general good times, one buzzing fly marred the ointment. In Utah, as throughout the nation, farmers and miners struggled in a post-World War I slump. Although industrial output increased during the decade, the number of workers did not. New machinery actually displaced many of them. Much of the increase in national spending was artificially induced by the new marketing techniques and was easily affected by any curtailment of credit. The postwar building boom had stopped in 1926 and the whole construction industry slid into a depression. Serious weaknesses in the international economy stemmed partly from the United States' favorable balance of trade. It became clear in 1929 consumers could no longer absorb all the products offered to them, and investment in American industry declined precipitously. The cumulative impact of slippages in consumer purchases and capital investment built an unstoppable momentum. Workers without jobs meant less buying; less buying meant less production and more workers out of jobs, and so on. Regardless of appearances, many Americans did not have to slip very far before they were facing real poverty. Income growth during the 1920s had been unevenly distributed. While a few managed unprecedented earnings, an estimated 60 percent of American families still had annual incomes of less than $2,000 in 1929.[16]

The stock market had reflected the other economic trends of the 1920s. A bull market which had attracted mass participation suddenly turned bearish in October 1929. Frantic efforts to answer margin calls rippled wider as investors raided their other resources in a futile effort to hold off bankruptcy. The most serious impact was on investor confidence. Before long all investments were considered suspect, and no one was willing to risk salvaged capital. By 1931 more than ten million Americans were out of work. And nobody knew quite what to do to solve the mounting problems:

> To the actors the drama of the great slump was as strange as it was terrible. It came to them out of the blue; they rode it as they would ride the wind. They were carried along by a course of events they were powerless to direct. Business executives, economists, and the public alike knew little of the industrial system they were operating; they were unable to diagnose the malady; they were unaware of the great forces operating beneath the surface.[17]

The effects of the national downturn were felt relatively late in Utah. In 1930 the state's commercial isolation delayed the depression's full impact, but markets for Utah products were contracting, and investment from the East was drying up. When farmers could no longer sell their harvests and Utahns began to face the same joblessness that their countrymen had confronted for several months, then many bankers and others found themselves staring into what First Security's Marriner Eccles called "the pit."

> During 1930 I awoke to find myself at the bottom of the pit without any known means of scaling its sheer sides.
>
> Since the crash of 1929, men I respect assured me that the economic crisis was only temporary and that soon all the things that had pulled the country out of previous depressions would operate to that same end once again.

> But the weeks turned to months. The months turned to a year or more. Instead of easing, the economic crisis worsened. The pit grew deeper and I found myself in it....
>
> Night after night following that head-splitting awakening I would return home exhausted by the pretensions of knowledge I was forced to wear in a daytime masquerade. I would slump forward on a table and pray that by a supreme act of will the answer would somehow be revealed. As an individual I felt myself helpless to do anything.[18]

Eccles steered his bank through the ensuing crisis, achieving one of the brightest success stories in Utah banking history, but other Utah banks had a different experience. While none failed in 1929 or early 1930, three did in December 1930, beginning a cycle which saw eight failures in 1931, fourteen in 1932, and six in 1933. The lag between the onset of an economic downturn and bank closures reflects the fatal pattern of continuous rather than immediate customer withdrawals and the cumulative inability to collect loans.[19]

Meanwhile, the national banking crisis accelerated between 1929 and 1933. The crash had a fairly immediate effect on some banks. During the previous decade, banks had increased their ownership of stocks and bonds and had extended an increased volume of loans to private stockbuyers. Accompanying the fall in stock prices came a 37 percent decline in bond prices between 1929 and 1932. Borrowers were finding it increasingly difficult to keep up loan payments. With growing weaknesses in bank resources, bank examiners began to pressure banks to tighten procedures. They in turn pressured their borrowers at a time when they needed more credit. As bank failures mounted into the thousands by 1931, deposits were tied up, depositors did not have access to needed funds, customers at other banks became nervous and withdrew their money, banks called in more loans and further tightened lending procedures, and businesses found themselves going under for lack of credit. In 1932 Congress responded with the Reconstruction Finance Corporation, which lent government money to banks and large businesses in trouble. By then, though, panic and runs on banks were spreading throughout the country. When the RFC was required to publish the names of loan recipients, citizens inevitably used them as a guide to weak banks and in some cases accelerated runs.[20]

Tracy Loan and Trust weathered these storms without ever approaching that fatal category. Russel Tracy recognized the seriousness of the Depression at an early date and quickly moved to keep his house in order. So the bank would know exactly where it stood and to make sure there were no potential problems which had been overlooked in normal operations, he began calling his men in to work nights. When they grumbled because there was no extra pay, he sent them over to a tailor for new suits. For further assurance he called in the international firm of Peat, Marwick, Mitchell and Company to conduct an independent audit. To buoy up investor confidence, he kept them informed of this and other actions. He began shifting resources to government bonds and other cash resources.[21] In December 1929, the bank held United States Government bonds amounting to $148,163. Two years later these had increased to a value of $247,720. Total cash resources had increased from $273,635 to $399,041. Customer business had also continued to increase during most of this period. Deposits grew from $868,832 in December 1929 to a high of $1,005,355 in March 1931. They declined for the next year but not steeply, and they were soon rising again. Loans and discounts also grew between December 1929 and December 1931, but thereafter Tracy began to slowly reduce them, shifting its resources to other areas.

Behind all of Russel Tracy's specific actions was a further strengthening of the conservative, frugal approach he had always applied. The car used by the property management department to inspect buildings ran through winter without a heater and with almost bald tires; but more to the point, the conservative attitude had always been expressed in the kind of mortgages the bank accepted: carefully selected, fully insured, income producing, in the best parts of town. When the Depression got to the point that no one seemed immune to its consequences, even the best mortgage securities did not matter if the owner had no money to repay his loan and there was no market for real estate. One would think that, to paraphrase Mark Twain's derogatory expression, one could borrow money only if one didn't need it!

Among other things Tracy's made sure that interest and taxes were paid. They did not foreclose as long as they were paid, regardless of outstanding principal. As late as August 1931 the company could note,

> The past 18 months have witnessed the extremes—fortunes quickly made and as quickly lost; uncertainty, fear and worry for thousands who have lost part or all of their holdings.
>
> With what we believe is pardonable pride, we are happy to state that during those 18 months we have maintained unbroken the *record established 47 years ago; namely, cashing upon request any mortgage or security we have ever sold, without loss to our clients of a dollar of principal, or interest due, and regardless of date of maturity.*
>
> *No client of ours had lost a dollar, or an hour's sleep, on account of any security purchases from us.*

However, in June of that same year the bank had to inform these clients that for the first time in twenty years the interest they netted would be reduced from 5 1/2 percent to 5 percent. To make sure the clients got it, Tracy put all interest payments on new or renewed loans after November 1931 on a monthly—rather than semi-annual—payment schedule. The bank argued that hard-pressed borrowers would find it easier to make the smaller, more regular payments. Similarly, in March 1932 the bank announced:

> Hereafter no loans will be made or renewed by us except with the agreement on the part of the mortgagor that he will deposit monthly with us, or some other bank, such amounts as may be necessary to provide a fund which will be used to pay the taxes in November.
>
> These monthly payments cannot be less than one-twelfth of the taxes and upon all such deposits made to us we will allow interest at the rate of 4% per annum from the date of deposit to November 30, when it will be available for taxes.[22]

By March, signs of the times were mounting all around Tracy Loan and Trust. In November 1931 the bank arranged with the bank commissioner to take over the safe deposit business of Columbia Trust Company, which had closed in December 1930. The Utah financial community faced almost constant threats of other closures and bank runs, but nothing matched the events of early 1932 which threatened to engulf Salt Lake City's entire banking structure.

Deseret National Bank was Utah's oldest bank. Its founding directors had included Brigham Young and other pioneer Mormon Church leaders. As such, it had long been seen, independent though it was, as an official Mormon institution. It had been a bastion of Utah's financial community, had received the patronage of a considerable share of the populace, and had achieved unmatched prestige among an even larger share. A sister bank, Deseret Savings, had been organized in 1889. Although not co-owned, the two banks shared Salt Lake offices, and the public considered them a joint institution. In early 1932, it became clear that Deseret Savings would fail to meet withdrawal demands. It seemed likely that it would pull Deseret National under with it.

The potential consequences brought Salt Lake City's bank presidents together to find a solution. Confidence in all of Utah's banks was at stake, but there were more concrete potentialities as well. Deseret National held the reserves of more country banks than any other local institution. The run threatened to spread, one way or another, throughout the financial community. Luckily, First Security agreed to take over Deseret National, merge it with another recent acquisition, National Copper Bank, and move it out of its shared offices with Deseret Savings over the weekend before the panic began.[23] When Deseret Savings failed, the city's bankers each had to take measures to protect themselves.

Tracy Loan and Trust never experienced a run on its deposits, which is in itself a tribute to its administrators' sound methods, but it also never took its success for granted. When the Deseret Savings crisis appeared, Tracy advertisements in local papers once again pointed out the company record of cashing securities upon request, without loss to the client, and noted, "Further, during the present anxiety expressed by a few, caused by the closing of a local bank we notified our depositors that we have enough cash on hand and funds immediately available to pay every one of our savings depositors in full immediately upon demand." This notice, mailed to all depositors on February 15, 1932, thanked them for their support of the savings department, as evidenced by their still-alive account, and noted further that

> in view of the anxiety felt by many at the present time, Russel L. Tracy as President, and James W. Collins as Vice-President, and also as individuals, wish to assure all our depositors that in our judgment we have enough cash on hand and funds immediately available to pay every one of our depositors immediately upon demand.
>
> Further, if because of present anxiety, any of our depositors withdraw their funds, and after further thought and more deliberation wish to return them during the next ten days, such depositors will not lose any interest, but we will treat the account as though the funds had never been withdrawn.[24]

It worked, and during the week of panic the bank's receipts exceeded withdrawals.

This was not the end of problems though. The nationwide panic brought requests from so many clients to cash in their securities that the bank had to end its forty-eight-year practice of repurchase on demand. Clients were reminded that the practice had been voluntary and that Tracy was under no legal obligation to absorb investor losses. However, although it would not buy back mortgages upon request, the bank expressed the hope and expectation that it would continue to recall any loans "which cause trouble, threaten foreclosure or loss."

Other measures were taken as well. In June 1932 stockholders were notified that dividends on common stock were reduced to 6 percent, and a year later, to 3 percent. Salaries of all officers and employees were also reduced. Bank resources were not depleted; the decline which had begun in 1931 when resources were at $13 million dollars had only reached $11.9 million by December 1933. But in the next two years, the slope would become steeper and a greater percentage of the bank's resources were tied up in real estate and in loans that were increasingly difficult to collect. Real estate holdings which at the end of 1929 had amounted to only $2,494 had climbed to $51,752 by December 1931 and to $124,081 by late 1933. That still does not seem like much when compared with resources of almost 12 million, but the largest part of those resources were mortgage loans which the bank had sold but still retained a financial interest in. When the bank's statements began to balance assets rather than resources against liabilities, as they did after mid-1934, and these loans were not included—$11 to $12 million of the balance suddenly became $1 to 2 million, and the real estate holdings loomed larger. They were still not unmanageable, but the bank became more and more involved in managing, buying, and selling properties.

In 1933 Tracy Loan and Trust founded an affiliate, the Local Realty Company, to handle some of these duties. Reports to the state declared that the affiliate company was "operated for the purpose of liquidating assets held by it for Tracy Loan and Trust Company and/or its clients." In other words, to sell real estate acquired from delinquent mortgagors. The property management department also became more important during these years. Numerous properties became vacant as families doubled up in the effort to make housing more affordable. Many other people had no place to stay at all. Tent cities sprang up in vacant lots and around the City-County Building. Employees in the property management department were kept busy checking on vacant properties to make sure they were not broken into or vandalized by people trying to get out of the cold. When a house became vacant, someone from the bank had to get there soon, or he would find all the copper wire removed.

Plumbing fixtures had to be removed and stored while the building was vacant. When the bank sold one particular piece of ground, the new owners requested assistance in removing a group of people who had moved on to the lot and built a shack of railroad ties and tin.[25]

Judging from bank records, large apartment houses and commercial structures were especially troublesome for Tracy property managers. Because of business failure or unemployment, tenants could no longer pay rent and frequently vacated. Landlords could not meet their obligations, including upkeep, taxes, and mortgage payments. Often, the bank had to assume management to protect its clients. In the case of large mortgages divided into participating notes, several clients had to approve decisions about applying receipts to various outstanding obligations. They might have to wait awhile before interest due, let alone principal, was received, but it was better, if possible, to avoid taking over the deed to a property than to face the prospect of selling it in the severely depressed market. When this was the only alternative, Tracy's trust department made a trust agreement with the participating note holders. Local realty began looking for buyers, and property management continued efforts to renovate and secure income from the acquisition.

A good example is the Stewart Apartments at First Avenue and C Street. This was a four-story building containing twenty-one three, four, and five-room apartments. Valued at $86,500 and insured for $40,000, it was mortgaged for $35,000. Tracy sold this mortgage in notes of $500 and $1000. The mortgage was due on March 1, 1933. On September 1, 1932 the mortgagor was unable to pay interest, and the bank advanced it to noteholders. Taxes due for 1931 and 1932 were also unpaid. Of the principal only $3,000 had been paid, leaving $32,000 due. The bank in November 1932, arranged to assume management. By February 1933, eighteen of the apartments were occupied and gross rental income was up to $550 per month. At this juncture, Tracy, again promising to advance interest due on March 1, requested that its clients approve a one-year extension on the loan. The owner had put the property up for sale, and the bank hoped that this would solve delinquency problems better than foreclosure. By October, Tracy reported receipts on the property of $3,503, most of which had been expended on repairs and operating costs. Interest was again advanced to clients in September, but during the next year Tracy was finally able to reimburse itself out of receipts for interest payments to that date. By August 1934, the bank could also report that 1933 taxes were paid in full, although those from 1931 and 1932 were still due. Client approval for applying future rent receipts to these instead of interest was requested. New furniture, exterior painting, and complete remodeling of some apartments had been completed to "assist in attracting the proper type of tenants." Tracy, which had been managing the building without charge for its services, had been unable to collect additional payments beyond the building's rent from the owners. Hence the bank asked them to "execute a deed thereto for the benefit of the participating certificate holders." This placed the property in a position where it could be sold without the delay and expense of a foreclosure, and it was quickly listed for sale.

In March 1935, a trust agreement was executed with noteholders. Some progress on paying delinquent taxes and complete payment of current taxes were reported; by October 1937, the bank still had not sold the building. At least it could report 100 percent occupancy and sufficient income to pay taxes and interest while still making improvements and covering operating expenses.[26] Finally, in December 1939, the bank announced that the former owner had arranged a trade for the property whereby he would be able to raise sufficient money to repurchase the property from Tracy's clients and pay the principal and interest due them in full.

This detailed account is an example of the unprecedented complications the Depression brought to Tracy's mortgage business. Throughout this period, Tracy Loan and Trust received no pay for its management of the property, although it received its normal share of the interest, when income was so applied. Similar circumstances existed in many other cases, and the bank had to scramble to protect its clients without incurring excessive losses of its own. Some compensation came in the late 1930s; as conditions slowly improved, the property management department eventually became one of the bank's largest profit earners.

The human costs of the Depression mounted as it dragged on, and employees of the bank, like everyone, faced constant reminders of the hard times, whether it was two or three families living in the same small house or friends and relatives who could not find work. On one occasion a bank teller saw an acquaintance of many years stop outside the bank and put on his shoes before entering. The man was from Bingham, and he informed the teller that he had walked barefoot all the way to the city to buy hamburger which was selling for 15¢ per pound because it cost 25¢ in Bingham.[27]

When Franklin D. Roosevelt came into office in 1933, he promised a New Deal which would address these tragedies. To curb the mounting crisis in American banking, Roosevelt almost immediately declared a banking holiday, closing all the nation's banks on March 6, 1933. Utah's banks had already closed by order of the governor some ten days earlier. Only those banks which could satisfactorily demonstrate their soundness received official approval to reopen a few days later. This action broke the panic, but much damage had already been done. Since 1929, some 9,000 banks had closed. While the Depression bottomed out in 1933, recovery was very slow over the next several years.

The New Deal introduced a variety of programs which strengthened and changed American banking. The Federal Reserve was given additional powers, including the power to raise and lower reserve requirements and to set minimum margins on the stock market. The Securities and Exchange Commission was created to oversee the stock market. Commercial banks were barred from marketing corporate securities and paying interest on demand deposits. The new Federal Deposit Insurance Corporation not only insured deposits but also introduced more rigorous bank examination policies.

In June 1933, the Home Owners Loan Corporation was formed to help homeowners refinance at reasonable interest rates. It purchased mortgages from mortgagees with 2 3/4 percent bonds and then rewrote them for longer terms at lower interest rates. Tracy Loan and Trust did not give up contact with clients who sold their mortgages to HOLC but continued to keep them informed about changes in the bonds' value. In 1934 the Federal Housing Administration was created to guarantee home construction and improvement loans. It would eventually take over much of HOLC's role and reshape the mortgage lending business.[28]

James Collins took over the presidency of Tracy Loan and Trust in September 1933, and to him fell much of the responsibility for recovery from the Depression. Although the worst dangers had passed by then, loans and discounts continued to decline until 1936, when they leveled off and began climbing again in 1937. The bank held more of these by then and did not sell them to clients. The bank's own loan assets started increasing in 1934. Tracy's balance plateaud by that year as well, and it remained in the $2 million range until mid-1938 when it again began a relatively steady climb upward. Most satisfying was the increase of 100.3 percent in savings deposits between 1932 and 1937. Moreover, these deposits were now fully protected. In October 1934, the bank informed stockholders that while deposit and trust fund liabilities amounted to $1.1 million, the bank had cash and United States Government bonds on hand amounting to over $1 million. Thus it could practically pay all deposits without calling in a loan. It also announced that, even though there was "little opportunity at the present time . . . to loan or invest money upon satisfactory securities" and consequently profitable investments for savings deposits could not be found, Tracy Loan and Trust would not follow the precedent of other Salt Lake banks in reducing savings interest from 3 percent to 2 1/2 percent. Russel Tracy explained,

> We are under no obligation to the depositors of other banks, and hence prefer not to accept deposits from them and pay 3% interest thereon, but we are under obligation to our five thousand depositors, most of whom have had little business experience, and who frequently call upon our officers for advice and consultation. Their average deposit is only about $200.[29]

This attitude of professional loyalty to depositors and investors, even at the expense of absorbing some losses, earned the client confidence that had helped stimulate the bank's 1920s growth, protected it from fatal losses in the Depression, and was now, in the latter part of the 1930s, pushing the bank into a new era of growth. By late 1936, dividends climbed from 18 to 24 percent of par value. The profits were largely due to growing diversity in Tracy Loan and Trust's business, particularly "the development and growth of our Trust, Property Management and Insurance Departments."[30]

CHAPTER 5

# Continuity With Collins, 1933-53

The Great Depression opened a two-decade period that brought unprecedented change to Tracy Loan and Trust, soon to be known as Tracy-Collins Trust Company, and to banking in general. As the 1930s waned, James Collins and his staff tackled the residue of problems stockpiled from persistent economic crisis. Of the many legislated changes in banking procedures, none had a greater influence on Tracy's operations than the Federal Housing Administration's program for home loans in 1933 and 1937. The stimulus thus provided was delayed by the outbreak of World War II, but the pent-up demand rapidly pushed the nation into a new era of prosperity, almost catching bankers and other financiers unawares. They fell into step with the new financial tools, techniques, and investments which had been developed but never fully employed during the preceding decades to manage a larger and more complex economy.

Tracy Loan and Trust's full recovery from the

crunch of the early Thirties required two things. First, loans that had built up a backlog of overdue payments on interest, taxes, and principal had to be cleared from the books. Many of these were large mortgages on commercial structures and rental housing. Besides the unrewarding commitment of time and money they demanded, they challenged the company's commitment to protect its clients from loss. Regardless of cost, a determination to do everything possible to meet that commitment remained, and much effort was put into winding up mortgages that were not benefiting from the economic recovery.

Second, the bank needed to stimulate its sluggish mortgage business by making new loans and acquiring new investment funds. While Tracy's was still the number one lender on real estate in Salt Lake City, it could not take that lead for granted. FHA's encouragement to borrowers was matched by Tracy's liberalized procedures for its many non-FHA loans, even while it sought deposits and other funds to apply to them. Although total loans had declined during the Depression, the bank had never swerved from the heart of its business—securing good mortgages. The dropoff had been due to the scarcity of adequate, reliable borrowers and to efforts to liquidate some of the more troublesome loans. Declines in credit capacity had been insignificant. Any loss of investors in the early years of the Depression was soon offset by the success of the bank's campaigns for new deposit accounts. In fact, during most of the 1930s, Tracy's did not send out loan lists soliciting more investments because of insufficient securities to sell.

Loans on large properties, which were especially hurt by business failures, increased vacancies, and subsequent loss of income, did not benefit from federal mortgage aid programs. The programs of neither the Home Owners Loan Corporation nor the Federal Housing Administration applied to them. Tracy had always advertised its ability to tailor mortgages to specific needs; but although it had gradually introduced such approaches as partial amortization, most loans had similar terms: three to five years with 6 percent interest paid semi-annually, and a single payment of all or most of the principal when the loan came due. Since many loans were renewed on this basis, the hardship of a single payment was not as great as it might seem. But with the Depression, the number of defaults climbed, and the bank focused on finding ways to protect clients from the high potential of loss. This usually meant not pushing the mortgagor into a corner so that the potential of repayment could be kept open while still meeting interest and taxes when due. When borrowers requested renewal, loans were frequently rewritten on more favorable terms, as long as some confidence in eventual repayment remained. As a result Tracy Loan and Trust really gained a talent for fitting mortgages to specific needs.

Much still depended on old-fashioned evaluation of a mortgagor's character and ability to repay, if not in the short-term, at least in the long-term. But once Tracy was convinced that a sincere effort to meet obligations was being made (and something more concrete than character was needed as evidence) then terms could be adjusted. Beginning in 1929, the bank put all mortgages on a plan of installment payments or amortizations, first on an annual or semi-annual basis, later on a quarterly or monthly basis. The option of full amortization was gradually introduced. Second mortgages, previously unavailable at Tracy, were now offered in special circumstances. Interest rates came down from 6 percent to 5 1/2 percent, then to 5 percent and eventually to 4 1/2 percent. FHA and HOLC encouraged this move by setting a competitive price of no more than 5 percent. Where possible, mortgagors were urged to use Home Owners' Loans. A woman who had a delinquent loan on an adjacent apartment house and duplex was encouraged to obtain an HOLC loan on the duplex to pay the delinquencies on both. Tracy Loan and Trust sold her HOLC bonds at $95 for $100 par value, absorbing the loss themselves, and paying back taxes and interest. Later, to reimburse Tracy's for paying the remaining taxes and interest and for buying refrigerators, gas ranges, and furniture in upgrading the apartment house, a new owner was granted a renewal which would be amortized and have a lower interest rate.

On payments on the principal, Tracy also worked closely with clients to suit their needs. On one occasion, it received payment of $2,950 on a $56,050 loan, and the bank notified participating noteholders that "there are a few clients who have lost heavily in stock speculation, are now in distress, and in immediate need of some cash. It is our plan to divide the $2,950 among those who really need the money, but we hope that you, like most of our other clients, will approve." Here, perhaps, some of Russel Tracy's and James Collins's humanitarian impulses were entering into their bank's operations. When a delinquent loan dragged on. Tracy avoided the not-so-simple answer of foreclosure, sometimes by ingenious means. One of the more creative cases involved the sale of a property to a new buyer on the following basis:

> We are to lend him $16,000 on the property covered under the present mortgage, which loan we will make. In addition, [the new buyer] is paying $2500 in cash and will give us title to 15 feet of ground, with a small building,

> some 30 feet north of this property, which we would take in for $7500 and which we can sell at this figure with a down payment of $833, leaving a balance of $6667, which is to be paid at $65 a month, covering principal and interest. The purchaser is a responsible man and we have a good report of his ability to pay. [The former owners] must raise $1300 in cash in order to make the deal, so they will get nothing out of the property, although they paid some $20,000 over our mortgage for same, and are paying this sum in order to clear the mortgage.
>
> This would make a total of cash received of $20,633, which would enable us to pay all of the delinquent taxes, pay you [the note holders] interest on your present notes to October 1, 1935, and return to you at this time two-thirds of the principal amount of your notes, with the exception of $299 which we would be short. However, we are willing to make this up ourselves so that our clients will suffer no loss. The remaining one-third of the principal amount due you would be secured by the contract of sale or mortgage on the property we are taking in, upon which there would be a balance of $6667, and semi-annual distribution of both principal and interest would be made to the holders of the notes from the $65 monthly payments received, on April 1 and October 1 of each year. Interest to net you 4 1/2% per annum.

Still there were one or two major mortgage loans that seemed to defy any solution and managed to give bank officers headaches for many years before they were retired from the books. The most troublesome was a four-story garage at 34-40 West Third South known as the Ramp Garage. At the time it was mortgaged, it was valued at $375,000 and was considered one of the more up-to-date, promising properties of its kind in Salt Lake City. It was at a prime central location, had space for almost four hundred cars, and contained a "superservice station" with complete auto repair facilities. Before the Depression, it had very large sales of gasoline and oil. There were also some small rooms on the ground floor, one of which was occupied by the most stable tenant, the Red Star Yeast Company. Tracy Loan and Trust felt justified in lending $125,000 on such excellent security as backing. Russel Tracy himself invested $7,500 in the participating certificates, having no reason to anticipate that he would come to call it "the most aggravating and disturbing of any loan upon our books." Other company officers and members of their families also bought certificates.

Trouble with the loan began when the owner sold it. The buyers had a falling out just as problems in the economy were mounting. After making substantial payments, they defaulted on the contract, it was cancelled, and the property went into receivership. By the time it was returned to the control of the original owner, the Depression was in full swing, business in the building was operating at a loss and rental income was less than half its former level—not enough to pay taxes and interest. Tracy Loan and Trust began to advance interest to its clients.

In August 1933, hope that this delinquency would soon end increased. Two "capable young men" with experience in the automobile garage business had entered into a lease on terms that seemed manageable even under current conditions. Sears Roebuck had just leased the old Walker Brothers Dry Goods Store across the street, which promised additional business for the neighborhood. Finally, one real estate man was working full time trying to find a new buyer for the property.

Optimism soon faded. In 1934, no buyer was found and income still failed to meet insurance, tax, and interest obligations. By August 1935, the bank had assumed management of the property. Income remained insufficient to pay the mortgage's carrying charges. Noteholders were only one year behind in receiving interest, Tracy had advanced two years' worth of that, and taxes for 1932, 1933, and 1934 or $15,233 were past due. The mortgage matured on August 1 and because of the tax and interest delinquencies, the bank could not renew it. Noteholders were requested to place them under a trust agreement, so Tracy would be authorized to take necessary action. It still hoped to avoid a foreclosure but wanted to be prepared if this or other measures to acquire the property were necessary. The only encouragement was a new lease with experienced operators which guaranteed a minimum rent and percentage participation in additional income.

Eventually the bank found it necessary to take the deed to the property. The mortgagor in the process lost his entire investment of more than $200,000. Tracy's staff continued strenuous efforts to sell the garage over the next years but without success. By 1939, they had to admit that this was one of the Depression-induced cases where they had been unable to protect clients from all loss. They continued to bear part of this loss and, to show their concern, particularly for clients facing urgent need for money, offered to lend those who so desired one-half of the principal due them at 4 percent interest, repayable only out of money received when and if it were collected from the liquidation of the security. A number of clients accepted; most others urged that the property be disposed of quickly without regard for loss. One wrote,

> Although this is the only trouble or prospective loss I have ever had with any of your securities, yet this has been so bad and of such long standing that it is like a single rotten apple in a barrel and whenever I am reminded of this it has weakened my confidence in all the good ones, and the quicker you get it off your books and out of the hands of your clients, the better for you and them.

In response Tracy decided to employ the daily reduction plan, which had worked very well with smaller properties but had never been used on such a valuable one. Under this plan, the garage was advertised at a starting price of $175,000 which was reduced $1,000 every day except Sundays until a sale was made. The sale opened on June 16, 1939. Finally, on August 15 the garage was sold for $115,000. After payment of taxes and expenses, a net amount of $104,546 was available for disbursement to clients, but in order to further share the loss, Tracy Loan and Trust agreed to absorb the difference of $10,454 and pay out the entire $115,000. Clients thus received 92 cents on each dollar invested. The bank was relieved to be rid of a loan with which they "had more trouble and worries... than with any other during our fifty-five years' experience." It represented "the largest total loss" they had ever had.[3] By then, essentially all remaining Depression-created encumbrances were cleared up. The bank had reduced its own real estate holdings, other than the banking house, from a 1934 high of $124,723 to $12. Loans had been increasing since 1936, partly due to the revolution FHA was working in mortgage lending.

The original goals of the Federal Housing Administration's creators extended far beyond making more credit available to homeowners and builders. Almost one-third of the nation's unemployed were in the building trades. Housing constituted the most important part of those trades. A program of easy credit for new home construction promised to stimulate the entire economy by increasing the money in circulation and the number of employed workers.[4] Although these goals were not entirely met because of resistance to the program by portions of the financial community, slow implementation by its administrators, and public delays in taking advantage of it, FHA made a significant contribution to the recovery. As passed in June 1934, it contained two important parts.

Title II was designed to revolutionize home mortgages to make it far easier than ever before for people of small or moderate means to finance construction of their own homes. This was done through high percentage, low interest, long-term, monthly amortized, and fully insured loans. Originally, FHA loans under $16,000 could be made for up to 80 percent of the value of a house or lot, a decided jump in the usual 50 percent of a property's value that mortgage loans were made for. The loans ran from ten to twenty-five years with monthly payments and contained interest of no more than 5 percent with an additional 1 percent for insurance. This was the cleverest part of the program. The government guaranteed the mortgages but did so out of the fund created by this 1 percent charge. As long as foreclosures did not exceed this fund, the mortgages were insured privately, without involving government expense but with the backing of government prestige. Two of the major causes of mortgage problems—tax and insurance payments—would be made under FHA in the regular monthly payments. Besides its general economic benefits, the need for such a program could be seen in the fact that construction of new homes had declined from a peak of 937,000 new units in 1925 to a low of 93,000 in 1933.[5]

Title I also addressed the need of modernizing or improving existing homes and businesses. Doubling up, increased vacancies, and general sluggishness in the real estate market not only meant that few new houses were built during the 1930s but also that few old houses were replaced and that the overall condition and value of the housing stock deteriorated steadily. During the 1930s, the median value of urban and nonfarm homes declined from $4,778 to $2,938. As late as the 1940 census, 46 percent or almost one-half of the then-existing thirty-seven million dwelling units were in immediate need of major repairs or lacked such sanitary facilities as a private bath or an inside private toilet. Under Title I, the government encouraged loans for improvements by agreeing to absorb 20 percent of the aggregate losses on loans under $2,000 made by any one institution. No collateral was required for these loans. The total government subsidy was $200 million, so $1 billion in total loans were made available. The success of the program brought a second subsidy of $1 billion while the government guarantee was reduced to 10 percent of the aggregate.[6]

While Title I gained almost immediate popularity and success, it was a bit longer before full advantage was taken of Title II. Construction of new residential units increased steadily after 1934, but did not break the half million mark until 1939. And while the FHA insured more than $2.6 billion in housing loans between 1936 and 1939, it had become clear by 1937 that something more was needed to accomplish the program's lofty goals. One of the first signs was a slowing of new construction in early 1937 which made it seem possible that the 1936 figure of 270,000 new units would not be reached. As 1937 advanced, so did a new recession which threatened the ground gained in recovering from the economic trough of 1933. Hence, late in the year Title II, a liberalizing amendment increased coverage to 90 percent of a property's value, lowered down payments, extended maturity dates, and reduced further the interest and insurance rate. Finally, the program was extended to rental housing which had been inadequately covered under the original plan.[7]

Many bankers and other providers of credit had hesitated to participate in FHA, distrusting such provisions as the unprecedented long lifetime of the mortgages until increased competition for good securities and the low risk involved gradually attracted them. Commercial banks, in particular, turned to home mortgage, as well as consumer loans in the 1930s to make up for depressed demand for business credit. Consumer demand recovered from the Depression more rapidly than business demand, and between 1929 and 1939 the proportion of bank loans going to households increased from 9 percent to 20 percent. FHA had a lot to do with this.[8]

Tracy Loan and Trust was among those which first hesitated. Its top priority lay in reviving its own loan program, always oriented more toward already-improved property than to home building. Besides, the company's success had been based on its relationship with eastern and local clients. Such investors were unlikely to accept the burden of FHA's long-term and low interest loans. These were purchased from lending institutions but usually in large blocks by insurance companies or by the Federal National Mortgage Association. While Tracy's clientele included insurance companies and other large investors, most of them were individual, relatively small investors. Title I home improvement loans, more suited to Tracy's operations, were more appealing.

However, increased competition for borrowers soon brought Tracy Loan and Trust into the program, though the bank would continue to emphasize its own loan plan for several years, incorporating FHA as one among a range of choices suited to individual needs. The growing involvement received a solid push forward in June 1938 when James Collins announced that Pacific Mutual Life

Insurance planned to invest approximately $500,000 in the Salt Lake City area through FHA-insured mortgage loans. Tracy Loan and Trust would represent Pacific Mutual in selecting and making the loans.[9] Subsequently, in the remaining years before World War II, the bank's advertising for loans under the FHA plan rapidly increased. The program, along with market conditions, also influenced changes in Tracy's other loans. Longer terms—up to ten years rather than the previous three or five—more installment payment options, and lower interest rates all became common. There was also a decline in client investment largely attributable to the bank's continuing struggle to find sufficient securities for existing, available investment funds. The January 1940 loan list sent to clients was the first that had been offered since before the Depression. Loan list mailings continued to be infrequent in subsequent years.

Tracy Loan and Trust seemed to be fully back on track by the end of the decade; in fact, it had never been very far off track. The Depression had troubled it very little compared with many others of the financial community. In 1937 and 1938, 30 percent of par value common stock dividends were paid out; this grew to 35 percent in 1941. In 1938 stockholders were informed that the trust department had "created more new trust business than in any given period during the history of our company." Renovations to expand working quarters, including a new directors' room and a conference room for the trust department, were under way.[10] Signs of a passing era came with the 1938 death of Curtis B. Hawley, long-time director, followed in 1940 by that of Frank B. Stephens, who had been associated with the firm longer than anyone except Russel Tracy. It was he who had provided temporary office space in his own quarters when Russel

Tracy first arrived in Salt Lake City. He had been one of the original incorporators and had sat on the board of directors ever since.[11]

In December 1941, as the United States was drawn into its second worldwide conflict, Tracy Loan and Trust reported to its stockholders that loan business had shown a substantial increase despite keen competition in the last year, that the trust department again had one of its largest increases ever, that the savings and insurance departments also had done particularly well, and that property management had continued to grow. Gross profits had reached a new high, but large tax increases for defense (another sign of the building international storm) had reduced the net substantially. A bonus of $12,000 had been paid employees in keeping with the long tradition. The fact that delinquent interest on all loans held by the bank and its clients—some $10 million worth—amounted to less than $1,000 was especially pleasing.

The federal government approached World War II with a victory-at-all-costs attitude. Deficit spending, which had aroused such controversy in dealing with the country's domestic crisis, was accepted as an absolute necessity in facing the international crisis. For those responsible for the financial side of conducting the war, the problem became not whether or how far the government would go into debt, but how it could be done with minimum negative consequences for the economy. The spectre of runaway inflation had to be considered in their decisions about funding programs.

Money for the war was raised in two ways: through increased taxation and through expansion of government credit by war loans, notably the well-known savings bond drives. Although it was well understood that the still weak and recovering economy could not supply all the taxes needed to fund the war, it was hoped that sizable sums could be obtained this way. Any tax income gained would both lessen the size of deficits and further restrain inflation by transferring purchasing power from the general public to the government. Congress enacted a wide variety of tax measures during the war, lowering tax exemptions, adding new excise taxes, raising tax rates, and increasing personal income, corporate income, excise, gift, estate, and excess profit taxes. One particularly important long-term change was the introduction of tax withholding in June 1943. Some 44 percent of war costs were paid through taxes. But annual federal expenditures increased from $9.6 billion to $95.2 billion between 1940 and 1945, so the 56 percent that was paid for with borrowed money translated into a large dollar figure. The annual deficit in 1945 alone was $45 billion, roughly the same as the total national debt in 1940; it rose to $229 billion by 1946.[12]

There were seven war loan drives during World War II and one victory loan drive at its end. Government officials aimed them at the general public, hoping that if people saved their money by buying government securities, it would help curb inflationary pressure by reducing purchasing power. Bank purchases of securities had an opposite effect by contributing to overall credit expansion. Some securities issues were restricted to nonbank purchase. The plan was not entirely successful, and bank purchases which eventually amounted to some 40 percent of government bonds, contributed to inflation.

Prices were rising at a rate of more than 10 percent by 1942. More stringent measures were required, and, from 1941 on a program of increasingly strict price controls was introduced. To further curb purchasing power, a system of rationing was gradually introduced. Durable goods such as tires or typewriters were rationed through use of certificates which could be acquired only after justifying each individual purchase before a rationing board. Gasoline and food was handled through coupons which either allowed purchases of a specific amount of a particular item or allotted ration points to various goods, thereby giving the consumer more choice on how to spend his or her quota of coupons.

Banks had a significant role to play in supporting the war effort. Their public role and community responsibilities had been enhanced in the process of dealing with Depression problems and consequent legislation. World War II strengthened this trend; it also forced other adjustments to changes in economic circumstances. Home building declined drastically during the war. Construction materials and labor were unavailable because they were devoted to the war effort, and, furthermore, the War Production Board in April 1942 issued a conservation order which curtailed further civilian building. As a result, demand for mortgage credit declined. Consumer and home improvement loans also fell off because durable goods were unavailable. Banks had to apply their money elsewhere, and, because the public had little on which to spend their money, banks had more funds available in the form of deposits. As a result, banks assumed a major role in financing the government debt and thereby the war by buying government securities.

Such purchases tended to heighten inflation, but banks can hardly be blamed. The government wanted to maintain the prices and yields for government securities, so the Federal Reserve increased its purchases of them. This increased bank reserves and credit capacity which, because there was little loan business, led to more purchases of securities. The government cycled the credit it obtained into general circulation through wage payments and purchases, increasing the money supply.[13]

Bank credit made an important contribution to the war effort, and it was, after all, the government's need for that credit which underlay that inflation. The banks simultaneously helped control it by "recapturing" much of the excess money in the public's hands through deposit accounts. They also participated in the savings bond drives, distributing the bonds and advertising for and encouraging public purchases. They also did much of the bookkeeping for the rationing program.

Tracy Loan and Trust continued to advertise real estate loans throughout the war, but, as with many businesses, they were motivated as much by the desire to keep their name before the public as by any expected response. The decline in wartime building meant that most mortgage business consisted of administering loans made before the war. The lapse in real estate lending, coming on the heels of the previous decade's mortgage problems and of FHA-influenced changes in loan practices, dealt a telling blow to the traditional company-client relationship. After the war, individual client investors would play a far smaller role in Tracy's operations.

The war brought other changes to the bank as well. As men were drafted or volunteered, women joined the work force in large numbers. The staff at Tracy was no exception. The bank had never before had a women teller, a job women soon dominated. Tracy understandably was proud of the men these women had replaced, and, as early as 1942, the bank advertised that fourteen employees were serving in the Armed Forces. Some were "among the twelve associates who have been with us for more than twenty years and, therefore, have life positions with this company." Before the conflict ended, many more would serve. Those at home had war-related duties like block patrols. One long-time staff member was pleased that he never had to perform his special assignment of delivering babies during air raids. But regardless of homefront sacrifices because of extra responsibilities, unavailable commodities, or rationing, it was hard to complain when friends and relatives were overseas fighting.[14]

Like its employees, Tracy Loan and Trust shouldered its responsibilities and made its contribution to the war effort. It sold war bonds and war stamps and in 1942-1943, announced the sale of from $5,000 to $200,000 in war bonds every day. Perhaps there was extra enthusiasm due to James Collins's position as regional director of the drives. Because many war-related facilities were located in the area, Salt Lake City was officially designated as one of the Western United States areas most vulnerable to attack. Tracy urged all those for whom the company carried mortgage loans to procure war risk insurance offered by the War Damage Corporation, a creation of the federal government. To its customers, the bank offered free brochures containing hints and suggestions for victory gardens, including vegetables recommended for Utah's climate. Another brochure explained the intricacies of 1943's new tax withholding and estimating law, calling it the "New Income Tax 'Pay-As-You-Go' Plan."

While the war cut into traditional business areas and placed added responsibilities on the bank, the property management department solicited business by pointing out that under wartime conditions, "the owner's normal rights have been sharply restricted by emergency regulations. Maintenance is a nightmare of priorities, shortages and delays. Taxes and tax procedure are increasingly burdensome. And always you wonder about the possible trend of values in the postwar period."[15] Tracy's property managers promised to take these worries and others off the owner's hands. With real-estate loans down, the company put new emphasis on personal loans, pointing out to customers purposes they might not have considered, to which these could be applied including real estate and income taxes, hospital expenses, medical bills, insurance premiums, emergency home repairs, education, and the consolidation of small bills. Even the bank's sponsorship of radio programs—something it had been doing for many years—took on a wartime tinge: on KSL, Tracy sponsored the drama "War Correspondent," while its KDYL offering was "Behind the News" with Meredith Wilson.

Of course, not everything Tracy Loan and Trust did between 1941 and 1945 was connected to the war. In 1942, for example, the company took out an advertisement in article form to announce that Standard Optical had completed extensive modernization of new headquarters on Main Street in a building managed by Tracy's property management department. Also noted was the fact that this department "represents far more downtown business property than any other firm in the city." Another source of pride and material for advertising was a loan made that year to a young man whose father had borrowed from the bank twenty years earlier, his grandfather thirty-five years before, and his great-grandfather fifty years before.

In September 1942 the Utah Attorney General rendered an opinion that Utah banks could not operate an insurance agency except through a separate corporation. Because Tracy was organized under state loan and trust rather than banking provisions, Tracy was not sure the ruling applied to them. But in keeping with a policy "to observe the highest standards of banking," it closed the insurance department, organized a new corporation under the name of Tracy Insurance Agency with a capital of $50,000, and offered 50,000 shares at $1.00 each on a prorated basis to holders of Tracy Loan and Trust's common stock. Officers of the new company were James Collins, president; E. Hugh Miller (manager of the former insurance department), vice president; and Eugene D. Amott, secretary and treasurer. While, in compliance with the banking act, none of the stock in the new corporation was held by Tracy Loan and Trust, all of the new directors were also officers of the bank.[16]

The most important event in the bank's history during the war years was one which symbolically recognized the degree to which the company now reflected the input and management of James Collins. On May 6, 1944, the stockholders officially changed the company name to Tracy-Collins Trust Company. The suggestion had been made by eighty-four-year-old Russel Tracy, and in his message to the board of directors he explained why:

> Forty-five years ago, James W. Collins, when only fourteen years old, became identified with the business of Tracy Loan & Trust Company. He is now, and for the past thirty-five years he has been, our second largest stockholder. His life and career have been closely linked in every way with my own, and I know he has become endeared to all of us.
>
> In our pioneer days, during his youth and inexperience, naturally he could not play a dominant part in our affairs, but for sometime past he has been to a large extent responsible for the remarkable growth, development and prosperity of our company, and I feel that the time has come when we should signally recognize and honor his

> contribution of time, talent, and fidelity to our business.
>
> It seems to me that the most distinctive way to do this will be to make his name a part of our corporate name. I deem it fitting that this suggestion should come from me. For nearly a century our lives, work and fortunes have been linked, and now it will be a compliment to both of us to link our names in the title of the company which has been the center of our energies and ambitions. Accordingly, I take pleasure in proposing that proper steps be taken to delete "Loan &" and substitute "Collins" in our corporate name, thereby changing it to "Tracy-Collins Trust Company." By this action, we will not only pay a deserving tribute to Mr. Collins, but we will also assure the company the benefit of the prestige and good will which he has won for his ability and integrity wherever he has carried on his work and associations.
>
> The satisfactory service he has rendered, the confidence and popularity he enjoys, attaches to his name, and when that is joined with ours, we will not only hold our old, but also gain new friends and patrons.[17]

There was little exaggeration in Russel Tracy's tribute to James Collins. Admiration for him in the community was so widespread that the presence of his name in the company's title could very well have brought the company additional business. One banker in town was known to say, "I'm convinced that people will pay another half of one percent at the Tracy-Collins bank because they think so much of Mr. Collins." His contributions to the war effort were widely known. At the time of the name change, he was serving as Salt Lake regional chairman of the War Finance Committee and had been recently selected to lead the 1944 campaign of the Salt Lake County War Chest. His community involvement was even more extensive than Tracy's. In a 1953 article, the Salt Lake *Tribune* reported that he belonged to seventeen civic, social, and fraternal organizations while directing or taking part in eleven different business and financial firms. His employees were among his most loyal fans. He had continued and strengthened the family-like atmosphere among the staff. They were encouraged to fraternize through events such as an annual stag party held at the Newhouse Hotel and weekly bowling joined by everyone from Collins on down.[18] The company had truly become—in fact, had been for many previous years—his as well as Russel Tracy's.

On May 17, 1945, Russel Lord Tracy died at the age of eighty-five. He had made his own substantial contributions to the community he had adopted in 1892, had benefited many people through his business, his philanthropies, and the numerous organizations of which he had been an officer or member, including Rotary International, Sons of the American Revolution, Salt Lake City Chamber of Commerce, Alta Club, Elks Club, University Club, Salt Lake Country Club, and several Masonic organizations. The *Tribune* reported,

> Close associates believe the Friendship Wall, a monument at his 1285 2nd Ave. home, expressed the affectionate philosophy that so dominated the life of Mr. Tracy from his boyhood through the years of business success and on to retirement.
>
> For Friendship Wall, constructed of 375 special stones, represented 375 friends, who had sent the mementos from all parts of the world. "The wall makes me realize the value of the many warm ties," he said on his 80th anniversary. Stones and rocks came from many men, now high in the world, whom he had helped over the years.

The *Tribune* further editorialized that "he was the personification of kindliness in all his contacts and connections, beloved by those with whom he was associated and honored by all with whom he dealt." And specifically, in relation to his business:

> Mr. Tracy was both a lenient and a successful financier who relied upon character more than collateral—willing to help but never crowd his customers . . . . he felt a pardonable pride in the institution he founded, which still bears his name and will remain as a monument to his memory.

The *Deseret News* also pointed out the success of his business approach in a lead editorial:

> In the world of business and finance, he won the reputation of being honest and fair in all of his dealings with his fellowmen. This reputation soon spread, and his business increased by leaps and bounds for the men and women who needed financial advice and aid learned to rely on his honesty and sagacity.

James Collins, in an interview years later, noted that Russel Tracy had treated him more as a son than an employee and that their relationship was "most remarkable. We never had a serious disagreement or an argument in all the years we were associated."[19]

World War II deficits were effective in generating economic activity and pulling the nation out of its previous doldrums. Unemployment evaporated and production could barely increase fast enough to meet the needs of an insatiable war machine. Looking ahead, though, economists feared that the war's end would bring another sudden downturn in the economy, a fear solidly based on patterns in the past. Hope lay in the public's accumulated resources, the pent-up demand represented by money piling up in savings accounts, savings bonds, and perhaps in the mattress at home. The dark side was that it also indicated accumulated potential for inflation. No matter how officialdom, economists, and business leaders looked at it, one thing was certain: American citizens and especially the soldiers were ready to enjoy a little prosperity. This demand and the accumulated cash to support it proved more than sufficient to carry the economy through the adjustments to peacetime production and providing jobs for millions of demobilized military service men and women. Inflation did result—prices climbed 34 percent between 1945 and 1950—but wages and buying power more than kept up with price increases, and most Americans entered a long period of sustained growth in their standard of living.

World War II had an enormous impact on Utah's deeply depressed economy. Utah's strategic location had soon drawn the attention of war planners. Its major cities sat at the nexus of transportation and communication lines, were located well inland and relatively invulnerable to attack, and had access to important resources and a large labor pool. Within easy access of rail lines and highways was plenty of space for military training, testing, and storing. The Army, the Navy, and defense industries located an exceptional number of depots, bases, and factories in Utah including Utah General Depot, Tooele Ordnance Depot, Deseret Chemical Depot, Clearfield Naval Supply Depot, Wendover Air Force Base, the expanded Ogden Arsenal, Ogden Air Materiel Area (Hill Field), Dugway Proving Ground, and Bushnell Military Hospital. These facilities employed thousands of Utah civilians. Because of the Korean War and Cold War, defense expenditures did not end with World War II. Utah's economy continued to benefit in a major way from the defense industry.[20] Utah thus shared in the expanded productivity and higher standard of living which began during the war and took off after it.

Americans went on a buying spree, and banks helped make it possible. Nationally, bank loans more than doubled between 1945 and 1950. Deposits also continued to show significant gains, growing by 17 percent. Combined assets of Utah banks increased from $199 million to $586 million during World War II, but loans and discounts only climbed from $70 million to $92 million. Between 1945 and 1950 assets climbed to $632 million, but there was a noticeable shift to loans, which grew to $234 million.[21]

One of the more significant aspects of the new prosperity was the popularity of suburban living. With the trend came large personal expenditures for housing, automobiles, furniture, and appliances, many purchased with credit. The proportion of home purchases financed with mortgages climbed to an average of 85 percent in the 1950s.[22]

At the end of the war, because of the two-decade lag in construction, there was an enormous need for new housing. One 1946 study claimed that from 10 to 12.6 million new dwelling units would be required over the next decade; this was possibly a third of the 37 million existing units in 1940. Housing units actually reached 58 million by 1960, but the incredible rise in cost of the average one-family house, which was attributable to increases in land values, building material prices, and worker wages, also reflected the inability of the supply to meet demand.[23] To help address the need while keeping houses affordable, the government expanded loan guarantee programs. FHA loans were still available, and by now credit institutions and the general public were familiar enough with them to finally put them to full use. More important in the first years after the war were GI loan programs. (Originally an abbreviation for Government Issue, *GI* came to refer to members of the U. S. Army and the programs designed for them). These loans were especially designed for returning servicemen and could be obtained with or without a consecutive FHA loan. Under the Servicemen's Readjustment Act of 1944, loans were guaranteed up to $2,000 by the Veteran's Administration. The guarantee limit was raised in 1946 to $4,000. These guarantees were not to exceed 50 percent of the loans, of which there were two types. Section 501 loans were regular first mortgages handled by the Veterans' Administration. Section 505 loans, designed for use in conjunction with FHA mortgages, were second mortgages taken on a property with a preexisting FHA-insured loan or applied for at the same time and normally used for a down payment.

Tracy-Collins was quick to take advantage of these new programs, knowing full well that the bulk of mortgage business in the immediate postwar years was likely to be with veterans. The first Utah home loan completed under the 1944 act was made by Tracy-Collins to Ernest Gillmore Smith, age 20, an honorably discharged soldier.[24] Marketing, like other aspects of banking, was entering a new age, though, and the bank realized that more Americans than ever before would become first-time homeowners during the next fifteen years. Tracy-Collins wanted to address the trend aggressively. Prospective borrowers needed to know both that housing was now within their reach and that Tracy-Collins was the best place to obtain the needed money.

Since all creditors could offer roughly the same terms, a wider program of reaching out to customers was needed. One of the best ways to do this was to help novice homeowners learn the intricacies of home construction, home improvement and home lending. A series of "letter-bulletins" was distributed which gave detailed explanations of everything from choosing a lot to designing a house to decorating the interior. Sample plans were circulated and "dream home" contests were held. One of the more important developments was to establish and maintain contacts with building contractors and realtors who would handle their financing needs through Tracy-Collins. These efforts were quite successful; one of the strongest relationships was with the Jensen family of builders, including Jacob Jensen, Jensen Construction Company, and Melvin H. Jensen.[25]

FHA loans were only one of several types of home financing plans at Tracy-Collins. A 1945 list of alternatives included "1. Straight loan with prepayment options. 2. Direct reduction loan—lowest rate—no delay. 3. FHA loans for building or buying. 4. Improvement loan for repairs, improvements or modernization. 5. Equipment loan for range, refrigerator, and other appliances." A wider selection of appliances and other large items were available to more Americans; they were an important component of the new suburban life. Home improvement and consumer loans, payable on easy installment plans, became an increasingly important part of bank lending. Individual Tracy-Collins advertisements suggested loans for purchases of such things as a new sink, a washing machine, a refrigerator, a new stove, a new car, a radio, or a television set.

Loan volume increased in the late 1940s while deposits actually dropped. Hence, the bank announced in December 1948 that it was in a position to once again sell first-mortgage loans to clients after the lean war years. These would net clients 3 percent per annum. There still were insufficient available loans, however, to compile a loan list. In 1953 the net interest rate was raised to 3 1/2 percent. These were thoroughly traditional loans, maturing in one to five years, completely serviced by the bank, constituting no more than 50 percent of the value of a property. The only differences between them and the first mortgage securities Russel Tracy had sold fifty years before were the interest rates and the fact that the loans were now amortized. The old continued to operate alongside the new in lending practice of Tracy-Collins.

During the war, the bank's assets had climbed from $2.5 million in 1940 to $5.0 million in 1944. Loans had only increased by $800,000, but government securities, which by 1944 amounted to $1.8 million as compared with $2.3 million in loans, picked up the slack. Deposits, meanwhile soared from $1.9 million to $4.3 million. Growth was substantial between 1944 and 1946 as the war wound down. This was the period when GI loans were introduced. Tracy-Collins assets climbed to $6.5 million; $1.2 million of that was in loans, which reached $3.5 million. Deposits also continued to grow, reaching $5.8 million. But after 1946, postwar adjustment trailed off as a factor in the steady growth for banking assets. Growth slowed for all Utah banks, including Tracy-Collins. Between 1946 and 1950, loans and discounts at Tracy-Collins increased by only $300,000, and assets and liabilities declined. Deposits dropped to $5 million. Recovery was rapid between 1950 and 1952, though, as bank assets climbed from $5.9 million to $7.8 million, loans from $3.8 million to $5 million, and deposits from $5 million to $6.8 million.[26]

In 1948 Tracy-Collins explained the savings deposit decline by attributing it to "higher rates paid by tax-exempt building societies and the fact that we have drawn from our savings in order to assign our clients mortgage loans." It was talking about the practice of encouraging clients to deposit the loan payments they received and then, when their savings accounts reached a certain sum, reapplying these funds to a new mortgage security.

However, the bank also moved in 1948 to strengthen its capital structure. It proposed to increase its common capital from 1,500 to 3,000 shares, or from $150,000 to $300,000. With existing preferred stock of $100,000, this would make a total capital of $400,000. The increase was accomplished by creating annual stock dividends of 500 shares worth $50,000 in 1948, 1949, and 1950. Each stockholder received one-third share a year for every share he already owned. Money for the plan came by transferring funds to capital from undivided profits, which were increased by reducing the normal cash dividend from $15 semi-annually to $9 semi-annually.[27]

Tracy-Collins Trust Company's officers in 1946 were James Collins, president; Newell B. Dayton, vice-president; Welby S. Emms, vice president and trust officer; Rufus A. Tracy, Jr., vice president and treasurer; R. Carl Granville, secretary; W. E. Shurtleff, auditor; H. P. Kipp, manager of the property management department; and J. LaMont Preece and Eugene K. Baker, assistant trust officers. Within a year, important personnel changes occurred. Rufus A. Tracy and Welby S. Emms left the company, and Samuel J. Carter joined as vice president. Carter's appointment symbolized the size of the company. He was the first major officer in many years not to have worked his way up through the internal layers of the company. No longer was it possible for all employees to work in all departments and climb a well-established ladder. As a member of the firm of Riter-Cowan and Carter, Carter had for many years, been the legal counsel for Tracy-Collins. General Franklin Riter, another member of the firm and United States Army Judge Advocate General, also had been associated with the company for several years as a member of the board of directors.

R. Carl Granville assumed the other vacant vice presidency in 1948. Henry E. Ogaard took over as secretary, J. E. Benedict became treasurer, J. LaMont Preece was the trust officer, and H. P. Kipp, H. D. Henager, and Blaine M. Simons were promoted to assistant vice president, assistant secretary, and assistant treasurer, respectively. The officers continued the Tracy-Collins tradition of devoting a considerable amount of their time to civic and professional betterment. J. E. Benedict was elected 1951 president of Utah Mortgage Bankers Association. Henry P. Kipp was actively involved in the Boy Scouts of America and was elected Scoutmaster of the Year in 1953. Newell B. Dayton was an officer of Rotary International. Henry Ogaard received frequent mention in the press for his contributions to several local garden and flower clubs. James Collins's community involvement was, as usual, impressive. In 1951 he was awarded an honorary doctorate by the University of Utah.[28]

Tracy-Collins had accomplished much as it approached its seventieth birthday in 1954. Its contributions to business in Salt Lake City were increasingly recognized. The Salt Lake *Tribune* mentioned an example in 1953:

> The Porte Press and Porte Publishing Co. (Tracy-Collins holds 100 per cent of the stock in trusteeship for heirs, employees, religious and welfare organizations) owes much of its continued success to Mr. Collins's efforts.
>
> For the late R. T. Porte had developed a secret formula for estimating cost of commercial printing. This service he sold commercial printers everywhere in the country. But just as success crowned his efforts, he died.
>
> Mr. Collins and his associates were able not only to hold the business together but to assure its expansion.[29]

Appropriately, Tracy-Collins refurbished and

remodeled its own building at 151 South Main Street. The mezzanine at the back of the bank was extended all the way forward to form a complete second floor, thus creating 3,375 square feet of additional office space. Although the vaulted skylight still provided much of the light for the second floor, new lighting was added there and on the first floor, along with modern heating and air conditioning systems.[30] Tracy-Collins stood on the eve of major changes in its personnel, organization, and business pursuits.

Tracy Loan and Trust Building, 1927

Interior of Tracy Loan and Trust Building, 1927

Directors of Tracy Loan and Trust Company, 1941

Mr. and Mrs. Russel Tracy
when they left on a trip around the world

Russel Tracy's Birthday Cake, 80th Anniversary

## Actors in Romance of Business

From office boy to president is the achievement of James W. Collins (left), who Tuesday was elected president of the Tracy Loan and Trust company. Russel L. Tracy (right), founder of the company, retired as president to become chairman of the board of directors. Newell B. Dayton (standing) was elected vice president of the institution.

Clipping from Salt Lake Tribune, 30 August 1933

The Deseret News

Salt Lake City, Utah. Saturday, May 6, 1944



ONE HUNDRED FIVE YEARS OF SERVICE are represented by Russel L. Tracy, left, and James W. Collins, right, whose names combined today in the new name of Tracy Loan and Trust Company, now known as Tracy-Collins Trust Company.

Clipping from Deseret News, 6 May 1944

First Utah home loan completed on service men's readjustment act of 1944. Left to right are Gordon Weggeland, Ernest G. Smith, E. A. Littlefield and Rufus A. Tracy Jr.

Tracy-Collins Makes First Utah Home Loan under G. I. Bill, 1945. Left to right: Gordon Weggeland, Federal Housing Administration director for Utah; Ernest G. Smith, returning veteran; E. A. Littlefield, manager of the Veterans Administration; Rufus A. Tracy, Jr., vice president and treasurer of Tracy-Collins.

CHAPTER 6

# Dayton's Drive Toward Commercial Banking, 1954-68

Any corporation that endures very long establishes a tradition or pattern, almost a personality, whose strength depends upon the consistency of the company's business pursuits and the stability of its staff and officers. Yet consistency must be to principles that allow adaptation, rather than to practices that change with the times, or it risks losing its market. Tracy-Collins, with its bedrock principles of safe investments, client loyalty, and community service, had adjusted to meet changing needs with a remarkable blend of caution and foresight. Most changes had added new services to attract a larger clientele and stimulate company growth. But Tracy-Collins also had a particularly strong and consistent tradition. Its personality reflected the long tenure of Russel L. Tracy at its head. He had also personally trained the men who succeeded him, James W. Collins and Newell B. Dayton, and influenced a host of other employees who either remained after Tracy's passing or learned the business from Collins and Dayton. Tracy-Collins grew for over eighty years under essentially the same management. Moreover, by the mid-1960s, at the end of that eighty years, it had lasted longer and grown larger without a merger or acquisition than any other Utah bank.

There are potential problems with such long consistency. An operation can stagnate, fail to meet the different needs of a different time, and find itself either offering something that fewer people want or unable to communicate with those who might want it. Sometimes only a change in status or personnel can push an operation forward again. There is often a delay when such a change occurs before there is real forward movement into new or bigger endeavors. Russel Tracy took a little while after moving to Salt Lake City in 1892 to get his bearings and establish himself before he incorporated. It took him sometime longer after that before he was ready to become, first, a full-fledged trust company and, then, a savings bank. James Collins took over leadership at a difficult time, in the depths of the Depression, but he had actually been responsible for day-to-day management for several years before that. Gradually, he shifted business away from over-dependence on mortgage credit toward a new and rapidly growing property management service, an enlarged trust business, more diversified investments, especially in government securities, and eventually more savings deposits.

There is some evidence that by the mid-1950s, Tracy Collins once again was ready for that extra push forward. The bank fully merited its reputation as a highly conservative financial institution with all of the accompanying connotations of being safe and responsible. However, its assets had not grown at the usual market-leader rate in the postwar decade of 1944-54. After doubling during the war, they had only increased from $5 million to $7.8 million by 1954. Although this was a 56 percent increase, during the same period assets of Utah banks as a whole grew from $480 million to $847 million, a 77 percent increase.[1] Tracy-Collins slipped from sixth to eleventh largest among state banks.

Part of the bank's postwar adjustment problems can be attributed to the bond market. The sudden demand for loans after the war meant that banks had to shift their investments out of government and municipal bonds. The 1946 decrease in the prices of bonds caused sizable losses for banks holding large quantities.[2] Tracy-Collins had a substantial government securities account, and the $600,000 decline in assets between 1946 and 1948 was roughly equal to the decline in this form of investment. A related problem was with time deposits, the only type of deposits Tracy-Collins could accept as a savings bank. After the war, a consumer-conscious public dipped into its savings accounts. From the peak of $5.8 million in 1946, time deposits had dropped off, and by 1954 Tracy-Collins had only managed to increase them once again to $6 million. Although these conditions stemmed from circumstances external to the bank, the argument could be made that the bank had been unready for the late-1940s and early 1950s economic revival and was not meeting enough of the community's changing needs. At least one vice president had told employees to be braced for post-war depression and retrenchment. The building boom caught the company off guard.[3]

This was the situation in January 1954 when James Collins, in failing health, graduated to chairman of the board, passing on the president's chair to Newell B. Dayton. Dayton had been with the bank since 1923. A native of Salt Lake City, he was the son of a successful druggist. He had considered following in his father's business, but a financial career became more appealing, partly because of a charitable old grade school teacher and principal, E. S. Hallock. While making a delivery for his father at the City County Building, young Newell observed "an old fellow with muttonchop whiskers" lecturing a widow about the advantages of thrift. This character, who turned out to be Mr. Hallock, had purchased the tax liens against the woman's home. To fifteen-year-old Newell he seemed like a stock character from a melodrama, about to evict the widow from the home she could no longer pay taxes on. "Instead, he drew a deed from his coat and gave it to her, saying that the taxes due were all paid up."[4]

Dayton was impressed enough to compliment Hallock on his generosity. He soon learned that this was a regular, though confidential, practice of the schoolmaster. He had in fact impaired his own financial condition while helping others: "He used to sleep out on a table at Saltair, and his headquarters were at his office down at the school." Hallock was willing to take on help. Thus, while making his own contribution to charity, Dayton gained two important rewards from the association. First, his part of the enterprise was helping to trace property records. Consequently, he gained an early and thorough education in abstracting and also learned his way around the County offices, becoming familiar with the recorder, the treasurer, and other officials. Second, he met a friend of Hallock, Russel Tracy, who also bought up properties and gave them to widows. He also developed a friendship with Russel, Jr.[5]

The preparation for a banking career that abstracting had begun culminated in studies at the Wharton

School of Finance at the University of Pennsylvania. With a 1922 degree in banking, he looked around for positions in the East but found nothing that aroused enthusiasm. He then received two phone calls, one from Russel Tracy and one from W. R. Granville, former treasurer at Tracy Loan and Trust and now secretary of the newly opened Central Trust Company which would one day become part of the First Security system:

> I came back and I went in to see Mr. Tracy first. He said, "I really haven't a thing for you to do, but if you don't mind washing windows and sweeping the floor—we need a good scrub job—you don't have to do anything, but I don't want to lose you. I want you to be on my payroll." I said I'd do whatever he said, so I signed up with him. Then I went to see Mr. Granville on First South and Main. Mr. Granville said he was so happy that the board had agreed to take me on as a learner. I said, "Well, I can't come. I'm working for Mr. Tracy." Oh he was certainly mad. He broke his pencil in half and went stamping around the office.[6]

His opening salary was only $65 a month, but the new banker was more interested in the opportunity to work with Tracy and James Collins. He, like others, moved from department to department, learning all aspects of the operation, but the abstract department soon became his major responsibility. He learned quickly, his skills were readily recognized, and in 1924, only a year after joining the firm, he was promoted to vice president.

Upon assuming command of the much larger bank in 1954, Dayton recalled the commanding influence of Russel Tracy's sayings and precepts. An especially important and oft-repeated one was "a moral obligation is of much greater weight than any legal obligation." Another which had a considerable effect on how the new bank president approached his responsibilities was that "a trust company is not built in a day but is so founded as to be nearly perpetual." Dayton would be responsible for administration of more than $40 million worth of urban Salt Lake County property. His intent was not only to protect and preserve such current bank responsibilities, but to expand into new and broader areas, further building the company and lengthening its life. He would in quick order move the bank into expanded real estate sales, commercial banking, and branch banking.

There were many similarities in attitudes and values between Newell Dayton and James Collins. They had, after all, worked closely together for a long time under the tutelage of Russel Tracy. They belonged to the same clubs and fraternal organizations. Both fished and duck-hunted. Their approach to banking derived from similar basic attitudes. Dayton's personal contribution to the Tracy-Collins tradition of client loyalty has already assumed the status of a myth:

> It all started... when a little old lady came in the bank to transact some business with Mr. Dayton
>
> When the business was finished, she looked out the door and saw it raining.
>
> "Oh, what can I do," she said, wringing her hands.
>
> Mr. Dayton's secretary, Beth Osborne, graciously offered to lend the lady an umbrella.
>
> The lady returned the umbrella the next day—and was loud in her thanks to the institution.
>
> Mr. Dayton knows a good thing when he sees it. He hied himself out and bought a dozen umbrellas.
>
> They are racked in the front window of the institution, and passersby—caught in a rain storm—are invited to come in and borrow an umbrella for free. To date, every umbrella has been returned.
>
> In addition, several people have seen the umbrellas in the window and have wandered in off the street asking to purchase one.

> "Which means," Mr. Dayton says with a wry grin, "that if anything ever happens to the money business, we can always make a living peddling parasols."

In 1960 the Salt Lake City Junior Chamber of Commerce placed concrete planters along Main Street. The next spring they were surprised to find tulips blossoming alongside the evergreen tree in the planter in front of Tracy-Collins. At first no one would admit responsibility, and the *Salt Lake Tribune* reported that for once, instead of a mystery vandal, the city was faced with a "mystery gardener." Soon though, avid gardener Newell Dayton was uncovered as the culprit who had surreptitiously brought a touch of bright color to the boxes.[7]

Dayton maintained the tradition of community service now expected of Tracy-Collins officers. In 1956 he was elected president of the Salt Lake City Clearing House Association. He served on the National Board of Field Advisers of the Small Business Administration, on the board of directors of the Salt Lake Branch of the Federal Reserve Bank of San Francisco, and as a director of the Downtown Planning Association. He was on the Utah board of advisors of Mountain States Telephone and Telegraph Company. He also sat on the board of directors of a number of local corporations such as Hotel Utah Company, and was an officer in many clubs and fraternal organization; he was especially active in Salt Lake Rotary.

On August 15, 1954 James W. Collins died of a heart ailment. Few men had contributed as much to their community, and innumerable friends, both within and outside the bank, mourned his passing. Of many tributes, a *Deseret News* editorial was one of the most impressive:

> There are two kinds of men. There is that rather

> small group of highly-useful men who make the world. And there is the vast majority of men who simply come along and live in it. James W. Collins was one of the former.
>
> It wasn't only that Mr. Collins accumulated a lot of money. Not only that, for no other reason than his own ability and dependability, he climbed from a $2-a-week office boy job to head one of the West's great banking and business empires. Not only that he was a familiar, respected and influential figure in the community's most exclusive business and social organizations.
>
> Much more than that. No mother can pause a moment in the Meditation Chapel in Memory Grove to remember a lost son, nor can any youngster marvel at the exotic birds in Tracy Aviary or benefit from the character-building of Tracy Wigwam Boy Scout Camp, nor, for that matter, can any citizen enjoy the benefits of the local Red Cross or Community Chest organizations, without unknowingly owing a debt of gratitude to Mr. Collins for the untiring, unselfish service he gave to those institutions and many others through the years.
>
> James W. Collins . . . was taken by a heart attack Saturday. Not often before has any man crowded such useful service into 70 short years as has he. He will be sorely missed by a community that also extends its sympathy to his widow and family.[8]

Newell Dayton was now not only president but the chief officer of Tracy-Collins Trust. His private mourning took the public aspect of expanding and strengthening the bank he was now responsible for. One of the first steps was opening a new real estate sales department in 1955. This differed from Local Realty by being like any real estate company rather than merely concentrating on taking possession and disposing of defaulted properties. Tracy-Collins was already performing many of the functions of the new department, but the reorganization put greater emphasis on real estate transactions, particularly large, highly profitable ones. The department was staffed with licensed brokers who could take title to properties that were purchased for clients. Robert E. McConaughy, Sr., and Robert E. McConaughy III were manager and principal employee, respectively. As with any realty company they advertised to buy, sell, or trade properties.

Tracy-Collins's greatest success was working as a representative or financial agent of clients buying important downtown or suburban commercial properties. In 1953, for example, the company handled the transaction which brought to Maurice Warshaw the land at Ninth South and State Streets where he would build a Grand Central supermarket. At the time, it was slated to be "the biggest supermarket anywhere in the West—including the Coast." The site was historic; it had once held the original Salt Palace, which had hosted such amusements as twenty-four-hour bicycle races. Later it had been part of a baseball park where the original Salt Lake Bees played.[9]

A merchandising revolution tied closely to the automobile and begun in the 1920s climaxed in the 1950s. Supermarkets and suburban shopping centers sprouted up across the country and downtown retailers scrambled to overcome their resultant deteriorating business. Maurice Warshaw was an important pioneer in the Intermountain West. In 1956, again with the aid of Tracy-Collins realtors, an even larger 62,000 square foot "one-stop shopping center" was opened at 3400 South between State and Main Streets by Grand Central Markets. The largest such retail outlet in the Western states, it was billed as the "World's Largest and Finest Equipped Market of its Kind."[10]

Robert McConaughy handled the sale of another

important, if somewhat different, property in 1955. Pipe Line Service Company, a national company with seven other plants across the country, purchased the structural plant of the Provo Foundry and Machine Company from the Thomas F. Pierpont Estate, for which Tracy-Collins was trustee and executor. Pierpont had been a pioneer Utah Valley industrialist, who, beginning around the turn of the century, built the company, which produced pipe, steel plate, all types of structural steel, tanks, coal pit cars, and other steel products into an important Provo-area employer. Pipe Line Service spent more than $300,000 to buy the plant from the estate and an additional twenty acres from Provo City. They planned, after an additional investment of about $200,000 to employ fifty persons.[11]

The McConaughys' association with Tracy-Collins turned out to be short-lived, as was the real estate sales department itself. In order to obtain Federal Reserve approval for entry into commercial banking in 1956, Tracy-Collins was required to divest itself of this department. This did not, however, completely end the bank's involvement in real estate transactions. It could and did still act as a financial agent or representative of clients and acquire land for them. The property management division or, in the case of particularly large properties, bank executives often handled such acquisitions. Revised articles in 1956 gave the bank the power "to conduct a general brokerage, agency and commission business in the purchase, sale, lease, and management for others of real estate . . . and to act as agent for selling, leasing, and letting of houses, buildings, factories, warehouses, stores and lands of every kind and description and the collection of rents and lease money and the payment of taxes for others." Blaine Simons, who held a broker's license, handled much of the realty work from the 1950s on, and after his promotion to vice president in 1965 he was in charge of real estate activities.[12]

The real estate department's activities, vital though they were, assumed secondary importance compared with other moves Dayton and Tracy-Collins made in 1956. In short order the bank obtained permission to open its first branch bank and then to move into commercial banking. Commercial banking meant a significant change in status. While the company had been a savings bank as well as a trust company for some forty years, it could not offer the varied attractions of a full-service commercial bank—most importantly, checking accounts. The Utah Bank Commissioner defined a commercial bank as "any bank organized for the purpose of receiving deposits of money subject to withdrawal upon check or other demand." Much of the growth in deposits since the Depression had been checking accounts. During the war years of 1940 to 1945, demand deposits in Utah banks increased by 291 percent while time deposits increased by 144 percent. Growth in both categories slowed after the war, but in the first five years of the 1950s demand deposits still increased by 40 percent while time deposits grew by 46 percent.[13] Savings would continue to outpace checking account expansion during following years, but Tracy-Collins could no longer afford to pass up demand deposit business. Checking accounts did not really become commonplace until World War II, but the convenience and security of checks was then obvious to schoolteachers, housewives, and retirees as well as the businessmen who were previously their chief users.

The change also meant that Tracy-Collins could expand its service and support of businesses of all sizes. In making commercial loans, it could simply create demand deposits or checking accounts. The completely revised "objects, purposes and powers" enumerated in Tracy-Collins's articles listed not only "to transact and carry on the business of banking in all of its phases," but also, the power

> ... to invest in or to advance and lend money on real, personal and mixed securities, on cash, credit or other accounts, on policies, bonds, debentures, bills of exchange, notes, letters of credit, or other obligations, on the deposit of title deeds, goods, wares and merchandise, bills of sale and bills of lading, delivery orders, warehouse receipts, warehouseman's certificates, notes, dock warrants, and other mercantile indices, muniments, or tokens, bullion, stocks and shares.

Or, in other words, engage in commercial lending. Tracy-Collins would also have hereafter the purposes, among others,

> To make, write and negotiate insurance of every kind pertaining to or connected with titles to real estate.
>
> To carry on the business of discounting and dealing in exchange, specie and securities.
>
> To act as agent for the sale and purchase of stock, shares, bonds, debentures.
>
> To receive money upon transient, commercial and savings deposits.
>
> To acquire, purchase and hold shares, stocks, debentures, bonds, obligations and securities issued and negotiated by any other corporation or association.
>
> To acquire by purchase, lease, exchange or otherwise, and to own, hold and improve land, buildings and hereditaments of any tenure or description.
>
> To acquire by purchase, lease or otherwise and to own and hold safety deposit and safe keeping vaults.
>
> To act in the capacity of escrow agent.
>
> To act in fiduciary capacities either by agreement or court appointment and designation.

> To borrow money and to issue contacts, promissory notes, bonds, debentures and certificates of indebtedness.
>
> To acquire, purchase, hold, warehouse, sell, assign, transfer, and exchange mortgages and deeds of trust, and to act as servicing agent for mortgages and deeds of trust sold, assigned and transferred to others.

Other changes in the articles, which were signed and approved on March 1, 1956, revised the capital stock, increasing it from $400,000 to $475,000 by converting the common stock from 3,000 shares worth $100 each to 15,000 worth $25 each, and changed some of the rules regarding the board of directors, officers, and stockholder meetings. Capitalization of the bank was actually increased from $750,000 to $975,000 by the change in stock because the new shares with a par value of $25 were sold for $75, increasing surplus from $400,000 to $550,000. Besides increasing capital, a major reason for the move was "to permit, eventually, a wider distribution of stock in the hands of the public." Further increases in the number of shares were planned for the future and put in place over the next decade.[14]

The increase in lending power and options and the expansion of banking services were important because they allowed Tracy-Collins to keep up with their competition, because they made branch banking more feasible, and because they opened the way to further growth. Tracy-Collins's main competition came from other banks, all of which in 1956 were commercial—offered savings *and* checking accounts—except Zion's Savings Bank and Trust Company, and it would soon merge with First National Bank of Salt Lake City to form Zions First National Bank. But banks as a whole were also faced with increased competition, especially for loans and savings accounts, from other kinds of financial institutions. One study of growth in financing between 1940 and 1960 concluded that "the most significant fact during this twenty-year period has been the strengthening of other financial institutions in relation to commercial banks.[15] During that time, the number of commercial banks grew from fifty-nine with four branches to fifty with seventy-three branches; the number of savings and loan associations remained steady at twenty-one, but their branches increased from zero to eleven. During the same period, industrial loan companies grew from 5 plus 3 branches to 110 plus 48 branches; small loan companies increased from 39 to 143; and credit unions exploded from 54 to 251. From any perspective, banking was becoming more competitive, and Newell Dayton and his staff were geared up to meet the challenge. Commercial banking began at Tracy-Collins on May 22, 1956 with the name change to Tracy-Collins Bank and Trust Company following in 1960.[16]

The bank's moves into commercial banking and branch banking were closely related. The application for a branch bank actually came sooner. Tracy-Collins requested a hearing to obtain permission from the State Banking Commission in November 1955. Approval for a Holladay branch was received on January 17, 1956. But such a branch would have made little sense if it was unable to offer checking accounts to residents and a full range of commercial services to businesses in suburban Holladay. The branch did not in fact, open until June 27, 1956, a month after commercial operations began downtown.

Branch banking had had an up-and-down career in Utah. Before regulation in 1911 a number of branches existed. In 1910 C. S. Tingey, Utah's Secretary of State who then had supervision of banking, recommended a prohibition on branch banking. The law passed on March 9, 1911. It can be seen as a combined result of the frontier's traditional distrust of all banks, but particularly non-local banks, and the Progressive Era's hostility toward monopoly. Between 1911 and 1933 this prohibition did not prevent a resultant trend toward monopoly—or, at least, that was a popular view. While branch banking was illegal, chain banking and group banking were not. In branch banking, all branches share capital structure and directors with the central or home unit. In chain banking, a group of stockholders, such as family members, hold the controlling interest in a number of banks with separate capital and directors. A similar situation exists in group banking, except majority ownership and control belong to a holding company. First Security was a pioneer in using the holding company approach to acquire numerous banks in Utah and Idaho. Inability to open branches meant that smaller banks were less able to compete with such large operations:

> The branch banking law of 1911 was very ineffective. The law not only failed to accomplish its purpose, but it created a monopoly for those individuals who already had substantial financial interests . . . In that branch banking was prohibited, it became almost impossible for bankers to expand to meet competition unless they had the outside funds to do so. The result was that a bigger monopoly was created than perhaps otherwise would have developed.[17]

The law also did not provide any greater security for customers. Not only was the cushion of a larger, geographically dispersed operation unavailable to counteract local problems, but where chain banking existed, the possibility that bank failures in one area could spread to another was still present. For instance, during the Depression three central Utah banks that shared management and ownership were liquidated, while a fourth was sold.[18]

The 1930s crystallized what had become clear to many who observed the rate of bank failures in the 1920s. The highest rate of failure was among small, rural banks in small locations with a small clientele and inadequately experienced or trained management. Utah had too many banks, many of them with assets and capital insufficient to cope with a crisis. Much of this "overbanking" ended the hard way. After 1933, the number of banks in Utah dwindled, but branches simultaneously increased. Small, isolated towns could still obtain banking service, but it would be increasingly provided by larger banks that had both a larger resource cushion and access to more effective, professional management. Any local risk of loss would be diffused over the wider area service by the entire bank.

Still, few banks immediately took advantage of Utah's liberalized laws. By World War II there were only twelve branches in the state, eight owned by one bank. It was the 1950s before banking came into its own. Branches were established by obtaining a new charter, by purchase of an existing bank, or by merger. Nationally the trend showed a market upswing beginning in 1955. The situation was similar in Utah where nine branches were approved in 1955, eight in 1956, and thirteen in 1957. While quite a few of these were in smaller Utah communities, many served the suburbs around Salt Lake City and other Wasatch Front cities.[19] influenced by "the rise in automobile production, improved roads and the resultant mobility of the population, the growth of shopping centers and chain stores, and the merger trend in industry." A 1954 study by the Comptroller of the Currency concluded that banks acquired branches "to increase volume of retail business ... to better service existing business, to follow customers to the suburbs ... to expand lending limits ... to excel in growth ... to improve earnings."[20] All of these factors were relevant to Tracy-Collins's decision to open its first branch.

Holladay was a logical location. A growing suburb on the southeast bench, it had not yet been staked out by any other bank; the closest banking facilities were at 3300 South and Highland Drive, while Tracy-Collins would locate at 4800 South and Holladay Boulevard. This was important since the first moves to establish branches in the southeast area had led to inter-bank battles that only the legislature was finally able to resolve.[21] The significant population growth in the region included a number of resident bank employees, including Newell Dayton, executive vice president Samuel Carter, and cashier William Von Elm, an added advantage since a branch bank needs to become part of the community. The most frequently recognized drawbacks of a branch were, "(1) branches lack flexibility and initiative, (2) branches lose close personal contact with the community, and (3) branch officers fail to rely on character and reputation in granting credit." In short, outside managers answerable to other outsiders remain aliens in the community. Tracy-Collins's strategy was to make the Holladay branch an institution locals could rely on to understand their needs. The first two branch managers, John T. Clarke and H. Thomas Davis, both were active participants in community affairs, both having served terms as presidents of the Holladay Commercial Club. One symbol that it had truly become a neighborhood bank may have been its handling of the customer financing for hookups to Cottonwood Sanitary District's new 1957 sewer line.[22]

The branch opened in temporary quarters, an old house at 4689 Holladay Boulevard, which was just east of the Old Mill Products Company factory and had once been its office. Work began at once on a new factory for Old Mill; simultaneously, the former factory was remodeled as a shopping center accommodating Tracy-Collins and several stores. The bank opened its completed branch quarters on January 25, 1957. The company's total assets had already climbed by $1.6 million in the half-year since commercial and branch banking had begun. The new branch's interior consisted of a walnut-paneled, three-unit teller cage, a steel and concrete vault, counseling space, and an upstairs conference room available to Holladay community groups.[23]

This building proved inadequate within the decade, and in 1963 a completely new office at 4707 Holladay Boulevard opened. Incorporating a large fireplace, lower counters, and more open space, the interior was designed to give a homey and spacious atmosphere to its 3,200 square feet. A drive-in teller window and a wood-paneled basement meeting room—again for community use—were other distinctive features.[24]

In 1959 Tracy-Collins sought another branch at 5900 South on 1300 East. For undetermined reasons—either the Bank Commissioner denied approval or Tracy-Collins dropped its plans before any ruling—this branch was never approved or built. But the following year on November 29, 1960, the bank received approval for its County Branch at 888 East 4500 South. It opened on December 8, 1961. Richard Baker, previously an examiner for the Utah State Banking Department, stepped in as its manager. Built near a planned new expressway, this branch also served the burgeoning southeast area of Salt Lake County.[25]

The County Branch discovered that one of the hazards of suburban banks was robberies. Two holdups occurred—in 1964 and in 1967. After the first, a local paper wrote,

> One trouble with branch banking in suburban banks is that they are the easiest banks to rob. In cities there are too many people around, and in small towns there are frequently so few roads out of town that they are easy to cover. Suburban banks, however, have fewer people around, requiring fewer men in the holdup gang and have lots of roads, houses, and other hiding places. Although the history of bank robberies shows that it isn't a profitable occupation in either branches or home offices, branches look easier than they actually are. After a recent holdup in one of the suburban banks, the branch manager of another bank got a joke prescription from a friend. On the envelope the friend had written, "To be taken after holdups and before retiring."

After the 1967 robbery, local banks increased security precautions such as employing plain-clothes detectives during open hours, installing surveillance camera systems, and training employees to better respond to the threat. Tracy-Collins's training included daily circulation among tellers of mug-shots of known robbers.[26]

When Tracy-Collins's officers applied for the next branch, they were less concerned with expanding into a new service area than with better serving an existing clientele. Their downtown office was hindered by its lack of drive-in facilities. Moreover, located in the middle of a block, it had no way to construct such a facility. So, in 1963, the bank looked for a location anywhere "between South Temple and Fourth South and between Second East and Fifth East." Newell Dayton explained that "the drive-in would be operated in conjunction with our main office on Main Street. We don't consider this a 'new branch' operation as such. We find it impossible to find adequate parking adjacent to our main office, and have been validating our customers' tickets at most downtown lots.''[27] While drive-in and parking facilities remained a major part of them, plans for this branch soon became more extensive than merely supplementing main office services.

Approval came on April 3, 1964. The location selected for this midtown branch was Fifth East and Second South, far enough away to insure that the branch, while relieving congestion at the main office, would have to be a full-service branch. It would also be an extension of home office operations in two important ways. The second floor would headquarter the entire Tracy-Collins mortgage loan operation. The movement of the bank's oldest service out of the main office was a measure of how much the bank had diversified, particularly since World War II.

The two-story $350,000 building opened on July 20, 1965. Designed by Salt Lake architect David Winburn, the steel-frame structure was finished with white brick on three sides of the main floor, glass and black onyx panels on the fourth, and a precast concrete window wall on the second floor. Two drive-in windows and parking service for forty-two cars answered the original goals for the facility. In addition, a walk-up window, the first in Utah, was provided. Inside, wood-paneling and high ceilings highlighted the 6,600 square feet of floor space on the first story, which contained complete banking services. The Tracy Insurance Agency was located next door in the same building. Upstairs were a lunchroom and board room as well as the electronic bookkeeping equipment. Thomas Davis moved in from Holladay as the new manager.[28]

In June 1956 Tracy-Collins assets stood at $10,171,678. Over the previous six months, as preparations for commercial and branch banking were underway, they had risen $1.7 million. In the month since commercial banking began, demand deposits had reached $2,324,716. In the next eight years assets increased more than 350 percent, reaching $37,014,916 in June 1964; demand deposits quadrupled; total deposits swelled from $8,894,866 to $33,769,020; investments in securities also quadrupled, and loans and discounts leaped from $5,878,578 to $20,804,523. The two-year periods after the Holladay and County branches opened showed especially large growth. Added assets between June 1956 and 1958 totaled $6 million, climbing to $16,192,888. Between December 1961 and 1963, they rose from $25,697,550 to $34,874,496, a $9.3 million increase. There was no comparable growth after the Midtown branch opened in July 1965. Although assets and total deposits did jump by $3 million in the last six months of 1965, there was a subsequent drop of more than $2 million during the next year. Bank officers were not dismayed. It merely substantiated their original contention that it was designed to relieve burdens on the main office rather than to expand business.[29]

Newell Dayton attributed the 1966 decline in resources to cuts in loan and deposit volume caused by customer investment in government bonds. In that year, vast sums went out of banks, other financial institutions and the stock market and into government bonds as bond prices "hit a forty-year low with yields at a forty-year high." Profits were still high: "net operating earnings were up for the year to $4.37 a share compared with $3.75 a year ago on an adjusted basis for shares outstanding." Dayton reported that it had been the highest earnings year in the banks's history.[30]

Tracy-Collins's personnel grew right along with the bank's assets in the 1950s and 1960s. In 1956, officers below Newell Dayton included Samuel J. Carter, executive vice president; R. Carl Granville and J. E. Benedict, vice presidents; Henry E. Ogaard, secretary-treasurer; J. LaMont Preece, trust officer; H. O. Voget, trust officer and comptroller; and W. E. Shurtleff, auditor. William H. Von Elm was hired that year as cashier and head of the new commercial department. Von Elm, originally from California, was a quick study in Salt Lake City banking. By 1962, he was vice president as well as cashier and had been elected president of the Mountain States Chapter, Robert Morris Associates, a commercial bank credit group. He taught banking courses for the American Institute of Banking and, in 1965, became senior vice president but returned to California later that year. J. L. Preece and H. O. Voget were promoted to vice president and trust officer in 1957. Mont G. Kenney advanced to comptroller. Preece's participation in the financial community included elections in 1954 and 1960 to the presidency of the Utah Bankers Association's trust division. In 1961 S. Albert Spalding became a trust officer.

Newell Dayton was elected chairman and chief executive officer in January 1962. Samuel Carter moved up to president. He also held another of Dayton's former positions outside the bank, president of the Salt Lake Clearing House Association, beginning in 1963. Other 1962 changes included the retirement of long-time auditor William E. Shurtleff, who was replaced by Ralph H. Webb, and, later in the year, another retirement by a durable executive, Henry E. Ogaard. He had been secretary-treasurer since 1954, and had served the community in positions as diverse as president of the Salt Lake Bank Officers Association and vice president of the

Great Salt Lake Council of the Boy Scouts of America.

Colonel W. C. McFadden, former commander of Fort Douglas, advanced to trust officer in 1962. Robert P. Jensen was promoted to cashier in early 1965. Ross S. Tyson left his job as regional administrator for the Small Business Administration to join Tracy-Collins as vice president later in 1965. H. Thomas Davis and Blaine M. Simons also rose to vice president that year. Davis became manager of the Midtown Branch on Second South while Simons was in charge of public relations and real estate. The year 1966 brought Frank E. Diston, an attorney and counsel for the Utah Legislative Conference, and now a Tracy-Collins vice president.[31]

These were transition years for employee relations as well. In one sense, the relationship between bank executives and staff was becoming more formalized. With a much larger pool of personnel at four different locations, a close-knit, family-like atmosphere could no longer be maintained at the same level. The attitude that each individual knew everyone else's job and could do it if necessary remained as a legacy of responsibility and helpfulness, but it was no longer a practical possibility. Tracy-Collins retained a fondness for encouraging better job performance through the use of Russel Tracy-style aphorisms. The Tracy Club continued to be a unique and rewarding aspect of employee benefits, but traditional company socializing moved to affiliation with the American Institute of Banking, the educational arm of the American Bankers Association. Management also encouraged and paid tuition for other employee education such as a course in public relations for bankers offered by the Salt Lake City Public Schools, and courses in advanced banking and trust methods at universities such as Northwestern University and the Pacific

Coast School of Banking at the University of Washington. These were also years when other employee benefits such as medical expense and life insurance were set firmly in place.

The look of the bank changed somewhat in the 1950s and 1960s too. In September 1956, a new, glass-enclosed entranceway was added, offering easier access than the old double doorway. In 1959 Tracy-Collins was offered as an example of a downtown business which had spruced up the back of its building on Regents Street; painting and other improvements had coincided with installation of an air conditioning system. In 1963 the bank kicked off a beautification program of the Downtown Planning Association by installing a self-watering planter box above and across the entrance.[32]

New conveniences and innovative banking practices were also part of changing times. The 1956 remodeling included a night depository. Bank-by-mail service was also introduced. In 1958 Tracy-Collins announced that it was the first in Salt Lake City to shift to "electronic bookkeeping" and 1961 brought the announcement that Tracy-Collins would be the first bank to offer "daily interest." The interest was actually compounded quarterly, but this was the first time a Salt Lake City bank had shifted to that system. Moreover Tracy-Collins was the first to allow a full month's interest on all deposits made by the tenth of any month. Customer convenience and public relations were served in brochures and advertisements in Greek and German. They pointed out locations in the Tracy-Collins system where employees who could speak the languages were available. Another pleasing public relations approach was the increasingly common practice of sponsoring art exhibits at the banks. Touring exhibits like one of Currier and Ives prints and shows by local artists were displayed.

But the most important and visible sign of Tracy-Collins's continuing "good-citizens role" in the community was merely its doing well what a bank should do—helping to supply the resources for community development. Some of the real estate developments in which Tracy-Collins played a varied role attest to the bank's efforts in this regard. In 1957 Auerbach Company, downtown merchants, acquired land through Newell Dayton and Tracy-Collins for the construction of a parking terrace. This came at a time when predictions of the downtown's demise were gloomily linked to inadequate parking. The plan moved the Salt Lake *Tribune* to devote a lead editorial to its praise. In 1958, Dayton and Tracy-Collins acted as representatives of the C. D. Stimson Company in the purchase and further management of the historic Newhouse Building at the corner of Main and Exchange Place. One month later, in May, plans for Salt Lake City's first major cooperative apartment house were announced. The eight-story Wasatch Towers at 200 South and Douglas Street would be managed by Tracy-Collins, who also acted as financial agent. Two years later, Tracy-Collins, as administrator for various trusts, joined the group of owners who would build the $1 million four-story Medical Towers building on 100 South and 1100 East, across the street from Holy Cross Hospital. In 1963 Tracy-Collins initiated financing of the first condominium office building in the United States. The building at Fourth South and State Street was to be called the Security Title Building after a major purchaser of space.[33]

In the years since they took over, Newell Dayton, Samuel Carter, and the other officers had increased enormously Tracy-Collins's size and stature. In 1968 Dayton could look back and note that during his tenure assets had grown from $7.9 million to $39.2 million. The bank had climbed from twelfth to sixth largest among all Utah banks, state and national. Moreover, it had grown soundly and honestly. Dayton could feel with his predecessors that he had helped build something that would last.[34]

CHAPTER 7

# An Innovative Edge: The 1969 Sale to John Dahlstrom, Gilbert Shelton, and Brooke Grant

As the decade of the 1960s came to an end, Tracy-Collins stood at a crossroads. Newell Dayton, the last chief executive trained by Russel Tracy himself, had reached an age that he wanted to retire. The direct continuity of management since the company's founding would thus be broken. Heir-apparent Samuel Carter, president of the bank, was seriously ill with emphysema, and there was no obvious candidate to replace him. Dayton faced the necessity of bringing in someone new to take over both top management and principal ownership.

Meanwhile, 1968 was an active year. The bank introduced its "Cashamatic" check guarantee card, adopting a practice which was sweeping the industry. With the card, customer checks were guaranteed up to $100, and the customer could draw on an automatic cash reserve. Young women wearing white caps with blue streamers visited city merchants, explaining that the card "requires no charges to or discounts from the merchants nor will it require them to open an account with the bank." Another new service was the Golden Pass Book account, a type of time deposit certificate requiring an initial $1,000 deposit which had to be left for a least 90 days and would earn maximum interest. The *Deseret News* noted that here Tracy-Collins, "one of the state's more conservative lending institutions has introduced an innovation in local banking practices."[1]

Several important appointments and promotions were made during 1968 and early 1969. Nick D. Lives and Ben F. Armstrong were named vice presidents while Robert J. Shaughnessy and Robert J. Alleman became trust officers. The most significant appointment went to H. Richard Poynter as executive vice president. The former president of the United Bank of Arizona, he came to Tracy-Collins in February 1968 with the responsibility of assisting in the overall management of the bank. Carter was, at this point, confined to his bed much of the time. Less than a year later, in January 1969, he would resign and Poynter would be elected president. Poynter had grown up in a banking family in Mound City, Missouri, beginning his own career there as a teller during the Depression. After World War II he had moved to Arizona and worked with several banks. In Salt Lake City he hoped to help Tracy-Collins contribute to the kind of vigorous growth he had seen in his Arizona experience.[2]

Newell Dayton was already in the process of finding a buyer. The careful passing of the torch to a successor who had been nurtured within the bank was due to end. As Collins had prepared for him and before that, Tracy had prepared for Collins, Dayton had brought along and built up Carter. True, Carter had not worked his way up from errand boy but had joined the bank as a vice president. He, perhaps, would have changed the continuity of Tracy-Collins anyway. Even more tellingly, he was only a few years younger than Dayton. The ending of the tradition was probably inevitable, but Carter's illness invested the situation with an intensified sadness.

Dayton put out feelers carefully.[3] He did not want to sell out to one of Tracy-Collins's big local competitors, a move that would threaten the company's separate existence. Simultaneously, he hoped for someone with Salt Lake City roots or interests so that the bank would not pass to out-of-state control. Could the independence and service tradition Russel Tracy had begun survive such a change? In his search, Dayton naturally turned to his lawyers at Parsons, Behle, and Latimer, working particularly with Calvin Behle and John Dahlstrom. Time dragged on. Several potential buyers fell through after initial contact and negotiations. The major stumbling-block was the price shareholders would receive for their stock. Then out of the blue, Dayton made Dahlstrom a proposal. Why didn't he buy the bank himself? Dahlstrom remembers that "until he said that it hadn't crossed my mind to do it."

John Dahlstrom, born December 11, 1934 in Ogden, was the son of Nephi Harold Dahlstrom, a grocery executive, and Marjorie Brewer, a health and physical education teacher at Ogden High School. After attending public schools in Ogden—where his friends included Spencer F. Eccles, later associated with First Security Corporation; Fred Ball, future president of the Salt Lake Chamber of Commerce; and Charles Canfield who would become president of Tracy-Collins—young Dahlstrom studied accounting, banking, and finance at the University of Utah, graduating in 1956. In the years that followed, he worked for the U. S. Comptroller General's office and as a tax law specialist for the Internal Revenue Service in Washington, D. C. He graduated from George Washington University Law Center in 1961 with a Juris Doctorate, was admitted to the Utah State Bar Association, and returned to Salt Lake City where he specialized in tax and banking law, first with Ray, Quinney, and Nebeker, then with Parsons, Behle, and Latimer.

Having represented First Security and American National, Dahlstrom was familiar with the legal aspects of bank acquisitions. His financial interests, however, tended more toward mutual funds and various joint ventures. Intrigued by Dayton's proposal, he defined the task as putting together the kind of "capable, competent, and consistent management" which was the biggest challenge of banking. Two men agreed to join with Dahlstrom in the purchase: Gilbert Shelton and Brooke Grant, both looking for a bank to buy. The thing most people noticed first about these three was their youth: they were thirty-four, thirty-three, and thirty-four, respectively. Ownership of the Salt Lake City bank with the strongest image of older, traditional management was shifting to individuals who would bring vigorous energy and a modern perspective coupled with an essentially conservative attitude toward banking which emphasized "safety and soundness." Shelton perhaps put it best when he called his banking philosophy "progressive conservative."[4]

Gilbert Shelton and Brooke Grant were, respectively, the principal in charge and manager of management services for Touche, Ross, and Company, a San Francisco-based national CPA firm. Grant had been a University of Utah fraternity brother of Dahlstrom and was a talented, well-educated businessman and lawyer, with a B. S. degree in business and a Juris Doctorate from Stanford, and was a Certified Public Accountant and member of the California bar. The three had recently collaborated on a consulting engagement for a company in which Dahlstrom had an ownership position.

They decided to acquire Tracy-Collins through a one-bank holding company which they would own. It would be called Western Financial Shares, later Tracy Bancorp. The next important ingredient was financing. Dahlstrom happened to be lecturing on oil and gas tax law in Vail, Colorado; his assigned host was an officer of Denver U. S. National Bank. Following a lift ride, the two, with their wives, walked down the mountain in the moonlight discussing banking. The result was that Denver U. S. National financed most of the transaction which brought Tracy-Collins to Western Financial Shares.

To resolve the pricing deadlock that other potential buyers had been unable to resolve, Dahlstrom, Shelton, and Grant made a two-tiered offer. In essence, stockholders could choose to sell up to 70 percent of their stock at a higher, premium price of $75, but if they wanted to sell all their holdings, the remainder would bring a lower price of $55. The new owners hoped to obtain 60 percent of the stock this way, but they ended up buying 80 percent, leading them to jokingly call their company "Western Financial Shares, and shares, and shares and shares." Purchase of a controlling interest was completed in early December 1969. The following year, Western Financial bought outstanding stock to become almost 100 percent owners of Tracy-Collins, resolving conflicts with shareholders who continued to request that Western Financial purchase their stock.[5]

The initial scenario was to hire a professional management team to run the bank for the owners who would continue their careers. But as negotiations went on, it became clear that one of the three needed to become involved full-time in the bank's management to protect their investment. Gilbert Shelton, the only one with bank operating experience, was selected. Shelton had grown up in Kansas City, Missouri, attended Yale University, served a term in the Marines, and graduated with an MBA at Northwestern University. After graduation, he began his career at Arthur Young and Company in Chicago, moved to the National Bank of Detroit in 1965, and later joined Touche Ross and Company in San Francisco as a consultant specializing in banking. Ultimately he became a partner in Touche Ross.[6] After a brief tutelage under Newell Dayton, Shelton was elected chairman of the board and chief executive officer in February 1970. During that time Poynter remained as president, but later resigned to pursue banking in Texas. In November 1970 Shelton took over that job as well.

Tracy-Collins had looked good to these three purchasers for several reasons. Shelton and Grant had set their initial search objective as a bank which was "middle sized, well established and with a sound reputation for stability." Tracy-Collins was ideal. They ended up going higher than any other buyers had been willing to go because of the Tracy tradition, "a reputation for quality." The bank's strong trust department, probably the best and largest in the state, was a major attraction. This sizable operation had much to do with the bank's growth in other areas, because trust monies had been pooled for investment, especially in real estate loans. Tracy-Collins's trust officers had not infrequently moved into running companies directly as trustees. The bank's strength and reputation had been built on the web of inter-connection between its various services: trusts, mortgages, property management, and so forth. These activities were, of course, especially directed at the "carriage trade," and the Tracy-Collins client was, if not necessarily wealthy, then stable, solid, and established.

Certainly, the new owners had no desire for drastic clientele change. They would continue to cultivate those customers while broadening the base. A larger branching operation was especially needed to take advantage of the city's spreading suburbs and to compete with other large banks in gathering deposits. This awareness was in line with a continuing nation-wide shift in banking philosophy from where banks made their loans to how they got their money. "Liability management" continues to be a major emphasis in contemporary banking. Besides new branches, Shelton and his colleagues began to develop programs and services that would appeal to a wider clientele.

The owners had other new goals as well. Tracy-Collins's conversion from a mortgage bank to a commercial bank had never really been complete, and commercial consumer loans had not yet reached desirable levels. In part, this situation stemmed from Dayton and his staff's long-honed skills as mortgage bankers. To communicate a serious interest in loans, the new managers felt they needed to de-emphasize mortgage lending and try to increase assets by 10 to 15 percent a year through internal growth. They established some criteria for possibly acquiring smaller banks. Shelton was also very interested in creative marketing and in electronic innovations. The two would be interrelated.[7]

The new energy showed up in multi-pronged marketing. Advertising was increased, even in such national publications as *Time* and *Newsweek*. But the main approach was new services. An especially important one was "Check 98." Marketing surveys indicated that one of the biggest irritants among bank customers was service charges. In May 1970 Tracy-Collins introduced its new account which required a minimum balance of only $98 to maintain a charge-free checking account. From about 7,000 checking accounts, the number of customers increased during some weeks by as many as 500 to 600 new accounts. In subsequent years, other new services included the "Double Dividend" plan where a customer, by maintaining a savings account of $500 or more, would receive free checking, the "Red Carpet Account" which offered a complete package of banking services for a $1.98 monthly fee (or free with a $1000 savings account), and the 1978-introduced "Tracy Accumulator" and "Tracy Plus" which allowed automatic transfers between checking and savings accounts for maximum interest earnings and overdraft protection.[8]

Marketing also included continued and strengthened support for the arts. In 1974 Tracy-Collins co-sponsored the "Museum Without Walls" exhibit, inviting twenty-one Utah artists to display their works on billboards throughout the Salt Lake Valley. In 1976 Tracy-Collins sponsored a major exhibit of works by the late western artist W. H. D. Koerner. Many of these paintings became part of the Tracy-Collins permanent collection.[9]

The marketing innovations moved in tandem with plans to increase Tracy-Collins's branches. At that time there were four existing branches. The West Valley branch opened December 23, 1970. But even before that, the main downtown office at 151 South Main was spiffied up with a $100,000 remodeling, transforming the narrow teller-cage-and-office-lined entrance hall into an open walnut-paneled room with wall-to-wall carpeting. Meanwhile, more innovative designs were being planned for the new West Valley bank which were completed

November 17, 1971 to rave reviews. Architect Arthur K. Olsen had departed completely from traditional ideas of what a bank should look like to design a building which from the outside looked like a large, stately home. The warmly informal, noncommercial atmosphere extended to the comfortable but elegant interior where woodwork and carpet made the customer feel at ease.[10] A new Sugarhouse branch serving another growing area of the valley was also nearing completion and would officially open in June 1972.

Tracy-Collins's quickest expansion came with its first acquisition of another bank, also in 1972. American National Bank at Fourth South and State Street in downtown Salt Lake City had been founded by shareholders and former officers of Valley Bank and Trust. A common practice in acquiring branches in Utah until 1981 was to found separate, independent banks which, after the statutory limit of five years, were then acquired by the larger bank as a branch in an otherwise inaccessible or difficult to get into area. In the case of American, Richard Wilde, president of the firm, had been a senior officer in Valley, and there were other connections between staff and owners of Valley bank. American National was a legal client of John Dahlstrom, and bank officers approached him in much the same way Newell Dayton had, asking him to help them find a suitable buyer. Might he himself be interested? He and his partners were. American offered a nice "fit" with Tracy-Collins. First, the midtown location on Fifth East was doing so well even after expansion that it could no longer handle all of the drive-in traffic comfortably. American's drive-in facilities were closer to the downtown business district and offered additional windows. It had younger customers than Tracy-Collins. Tracy-Collins had more commercial loan business.[11]

By November 1971, holders of 95 percent of American National's stock had agreed to Tracy's offer, but approval from various regulatory agencies—American was a national bank, Tracy-Collins a state—took longer. Tracy paid $2,428,000 for the merger, seventy dollars a share of which $1,899,000 was in cash for the bank's nonreal-estate capital. Another $20 a share was represented as stock in the wholly-owned real estate company which owned the bank's buildings. With American National's $24 million in resources, Tracy-Collins's total climbed to $103 million. In addition to American's home office, Tracy-Collins acquired its one branch in Midvale at 7095 South State Street.[12]

Six months after completing the American National deal, in June 1972, Tracy-Collins officers were bidding for a second acquisition. This time the target was Farmers State Bank of Woods Cross. Shelton and his partners jumped at the chance to move into potentially lucrative Davis County when they heard the bank just west of Bountiful might be on the market. The Farmers Board released a letter to stockholders describing the tentative offer. Close to 50 percent of the stockholders tendered their stock. Farmers's management reconsidered and within thirty days virtually 100 percent of the stock came in. Tracy-Collins paid $2.5 million dollars for Farmers's $1.4 million book value, taking over in September 1974. An additional $21.7 million in Farmers resources brought Tracy-Collins resources to $132 million.

Despite some contesting of these acquisitions and despite regulatory delays, both purchases went relatively smoothly. There are, however, always some problems in small-large mergers. They make loans by different standards. For example, a small, local bank like Farmers often has different loan policies and rates. By allowing a step-by-step process to bring Farmers into line with its new owner's procedures and policies, both were soon operating smoothly as branches in the Tracy-Collins system.[13]

The Tracy-Collins tree sprouted other branches during the 1970s. In 1972 Tracy-Collins filed for a branch at the new Snowbird Resort in Little Cottonwood Canyon. This branch, including a 24-hour Cashamatic unit, opened on January 24, 1974. On July 3, 1975,the Cottonwood branch at 4900 Highland Drive opened before a festive gathering entertained by fireworks, a nineteen-round salute from the Mountain Men of the Wasatch, singing by Robert Peterson, and flag hoisting by Governor Calvin Rampton.[14] North Salt Lake and Sandy branches opened in October 1977 and October 1978, respectively. The Foothill and West Jordan branches followed in February 1979.

The most notable aspect of Tracy-Collins branching during the seventies concerned its pioneer role in acquiring and setting up automated teller machines, commonly known as ATMs. Electronic banking was a fascination of Shelton's. He had specialized in business engineering and in time-and-motion study approaches, been a consultant with Master Card, kept up on innovations such as electronic funds transfers and automated teller machines, and at the National Bank of Detroit, had operated a twenty-four hour, seven-day-a-week computer operation. The partners decided Tracy-Collins was ready. He and Dahlstrom visited with the founders of Docutel, who would supply the ATMs, and they decided on what was for Salt Lake City a revolutionary approach. They would not limit themselves to adding ATMs to the outside of branch buildings. Instead they would seek approval to build stand-alone ATM branches at multiple locations in Salt Lake Valley. That way, instead of having to build a $400,000 building for a branch, they could erect a $45-to-60,000 stand-alone teller. In late 1971 they applied to the Utah Department of Financial Institutions for ten such "branches." Executive Vice President Ronald Carnago was delighted that 95 percent of the previous transactions handled by human tellers could now be handled by machines:

> These include deposits or withdrawals from checking or savings accounts, transfer of funds between accounts, the dispensing of cash from checking, credit card or savings accounts.
>
> The customer makes his [or her] identity known to the machine with a card containing a magnetic stripe. The stripe has an invisible coding that identifies the holder and states his [or her] credit limitation.
>
> The holder verifies ownership by punching into the machine's keyboard a four-digit code number known only to the individual. This prevents the use of the card by anyone other than the owner.
>
> The machine gives the holder three chances to punch in the proper code number. If he [or she] is incorrect on the third try, the machine "swallows" the card. The holder is then advised by lighted instructions to contact the branch manager.
>
> Cash is dispensed—along with a memo for the customer's records—in increments of $10 bills. Total amount of cash issued in any one day to a customer is limited by a previously assigned credit designation.
>
> A withdrawal at any one machine is recorded by central computer. Hence the credit limitation remains firm even if a customer makes a withdrawal at another or sequence of machine locations.[15]

The idea was not universally admired. In fact, Utah's conservative banking community was distinctly hostile. Accusations of banking-by-"coke-machine" or "vending-machine" circulated. There was negative pressure by a number of banks before Commissioner of Financial Institutions Smoot Brimhall made his decision; clearly though cautiously, in March 1972, he authorized construction of the first Tracy-Collins stand-alone teller, this one at the Salt Lake City International Airport. Tracy-Collins installed ATMs at existing branches and built two more stand-alone machines as approval came in 1972; one at Carriage Square and one at Union Square.

The machines became a major marketing breakthrough for Tracy-Collins which was soon advertising as "The Bank That Is Always Open." In 1974, the *Deseret News* reported that "automatic teller machines are proving quite popular among bank customers because of the convenience of drawing out cash at any hour. And the added gush of business is just as popular with the banks."[16]

Other electronic advances soon followed. Based on his experience at the National Bank of Detroit, Shelton took a new look at Tracy-Collins's own computer operation. He decided that the bank wasn't big enough to keep on top of what was happening in the computer industry by hiring its own systems people and programmers. It seemed better to go with a company that was already working with several banks, one that had suitable programs already available, but also the talent to design programs to fit Tracy-Collins's needs. Systematics Corporation of Little Rock, Arkansas, was selected and helped Tracy-Collins set up the first on-line teller system in Salt Lake City, later also making Tracy-Collins the first bank to put its trust department on-line. In 1979 construction began on a $1.5 million operations and computer center for Tracy-Collins in Yates Industrial Park to house sixty-seven Tracy-Collins and twenty Systematics employees.[17]

New facilities were not limited to new branches or ATMs. In 1974 the home office of Tracy-Collins moved into a renovated building on the corner of Main and First South, a location which officers still consider the best in the city. The former Montgomery Ward building was constructed in 1937 "neo-Georgian" style as interpreted by Raymond Evans and Raymond Ashton. Previously, the corner had been the site of the Godbe-Pitts building, containing a drug store, a succession of taverns, and other small businesses. Before Shelton and Dahlstrom purchased it, the Montgomery Ward building had for several years housed the genealogical library of The Church of Jesus Christ of Latter-day Saints. Plans included converting the building into a complete financial services center containing brokerage houses and other financial firms as well as the banks. The architects added two-story windows, according to design by Architects John Earl Warneke and Lloyd Snedaker, of the type used in the reconstruction of the U. S. Court of Claims Building in Washington, D. C. The roof was raised by two feet to accommodate a fourth floor which had been contemplated in the original design. The Utah Heritage Foundation commended Tracy-Collins on its preservation of the building when the new facility opened on August 29, 1974. Official ceremonies, held September 3, included a display of art by the twenty-one artists who had participated in the "Museum Without Walls" exhibit. The old building at 151 South Main was sold in December, but one notable part of it had gone to the new quarters: its 1916 vintage twelve-ton and six-ton vault doors which had an estimated value of half a million dollars.[18]

Tracy-Collins was growing rapidly, thanks in part to the establishment of a strong commercial loan department. The bank worked closely with the Small Business

Administration and, following much the same pattern as Russel Tracy's with mortgages, concentrated on selling out loans to keep capital turnover high and bring new funds into a capital-poor state. During the early years after the 1969 purchase, Tracy-Collins had cut back on its mortgage lending. The new owners had felt that the bank had an excessive number of low-yielding loans; so they decided to let these amortize. After two or three years it became clear that Salt Lake City was experiencing a dynamic housing spurt. Consequently, the bank decided to re-enter the field of real estate loans in a big way, but a separate subsidiary, Tracy Mortgage, would handle most of the business. Since most banks had a real estate department, this was an innovation—one that tremendously increased the company's ability to buy and sell loans by dealing with other mortgage or savings and loan companies. In the rivalry traditional among financial institutions, banks normally deal with other banks rather than with mortgage companies, while mortgage companies reciprocate. Savings and loan companies prefer to work with a mortgage company, even if owned by a bank, rather than with the bank itself. While Tracy Mortgage continued to use its bank's facility just as if it were a department, it financed its own mortgages and developed a broader market than otherwise possible, a genuine advantage since banks were not, at that boom time, selling term loans to each other.[19]

Tracy-Collins's phenomenal growth during the 1970s can be traced in the statistics. In December 1969 the bank's total resources were $45,141,550. By mid-1972 these had already swelled to $104,617,427, and by mid-1980, a little more than ten years after Shelton, Dahlstrom, and Grant had bought the bank, assets had grown to $204,650,000. During the same ten and a half years, demand deposits had increased from $15,543,306 to $54,140,000, time deposits from $22,614,349 to $119,854,000, and loans and discounts from $24,387,274 to $116,809,000.

Such growth was also reflected in personnel. One of the most important additions to senior executive positions was Charles Canfield, eventually Tracy-Collins's president. Canfield had grown up in the banking business, working with his father, who had established numerous banks throughout the West. In 1963 the two, with others, founded the Bank of Commerce in Magna, Utah. In 1970 the Canfields and others sold the bank to Zions First National Bank. The younger Canfield considered joining the staff at Zions, but in the meantime he ran into childhood friend John Dahlstrom, who, in turn, introduced him to Gilbert Shelton. Canfield hired on at Tracy-Collins, graduating rapidly through a series of important positions to senior vice president, executive vice president, and eventually, president. He is given much of the credit for strengthening Tracy-Collins's commercial loan and real estate loan operations. Ben Armstrong, who joined the bank in 1965, was also especially important to the Commercial Loan Division, the operation of which has involved minimal losses over an extended period.

John Cooper and Ted May had much to do with the revival of real estate lending. A leading mortgage banker in the region, Cooper organized the Tracy Mortgage Company. Along with Cooper, the executive vice president and president of Tracy Mortgage as this history is being written, May was initially a builder, head of the Salt Lake County Planning and Zoning Department, and used common sense and good judgment in ways that were invaluable to the overall bank organization. Frank

Diston, executive vice president and head of the Trust Department, has been with the bank since 1966. He is responsible for the high respect accorded the Trust Department throughout the Intermountain West.[20] The wide range of Tracy-Collins experience at the time of this centennial appraisal is suggested by the fact that fourteen employees have been associated with the bank for more than twenty years.[21]

The most remarkable of these, perhaps, is Blaine M. Simons, who has worked with Tracy-Collins in marketing and business development for more than fifty years. Oriented to the needs of customers, he has effectively built Tracy-Collins's reputation as "a people's bank."

Two more recent figures who had extensive public lives beyond their work at the bank and helped bring the bank considerable attention were Joseph Peery and Vee Carlisle. Peery, named economist for Tracy-Collins in 1970, was a professor in the University of Utah's College of Business, an important advisor to the bank's officers, and publisher of the *Tracy Trend-Letter*, an influential periodical which drew national attention. In 1971 Vee Carlisle joined the bank as head of the Consumer Services Division, also known as the Women's Division. From this position she exercised a great deal of influence in encouraging women in business and banking careers and in helping them manage their finances. Her division sponsored numerous programs, seminars, and community events, but perhaps its most useful service was working in conjunction with Welcome Wagon to help newcomers adjust to their new homes in Salt Lake City. Before arriving in Salt Lake City, women in moving families received a newcomers' information kit from Tracy-Collins. The kit contained virtually everything anyone would want to know about moving and living in the new environment, from recreation to housing to financial services to state laws. It, of course, also helped bring Tracy-Collins new accounts.[22]

After helping to put Tracy-Collins Bank and Trust at the local forefront in banking innovations and steering it along a course of remarkable growth, Gilbert Shelton decided in 1982 to sell out his interest. As the one of the three owners who had been the day-to-day manager, he had each year received a large stock bonus. By the early 1980s he had earned all the incentives available. It was not possible to gain a further ownership position without buying out his partners; alternatively he could realize his bonuses by selling out. He made his choice, largely, he says, because he no longer felt a continual challenge in running the bank. According to Shelton, innovations were severely curtailed by the enormous increase in government supervision and regulation, and banking no longer seemed to be headed in an appealing direction. Returning to San Francisco, he left Tracy-Collins in the capable hands of John Dahlstrom as chairman of the board and "Chuck" Canfield as president, with the remaining management team in place.

Tracy-Collins Trust Building, in 1950s

James W. Collins

Newell B. Dayton

John Dahlstrom, Chairman

C. R. Canfield, President

Left to right: Brooke Grant, Gil Shelton, John Dahlstrom

John and Marylin Dahlstrom, Chairman of the Board and Director, respectively, of Tracy-Collins in 1984.

# Members of the Board of Directors of Tracy-Collins Bank and Trust Company, 1984

**John A. Dahlstrom**
Chairman of the Board

**C. R. Canfield**
Vice Chairman and President

**Ted May**
President, Tracy Mortgage Co. & Executive Vice President Tracy Collins Bank

**Ben F. Armstrong**
Executive Vice President
Commercial Lending

**James E. Brown**
Executive
Thiokol Corporation

**Mac Christensen**
President
Mac's Clothing Inc.

**Richard A. Christenson**
President
First Security Financial

**Dale R. Curtis**
Chairman, Employee
Benefit Specialist Inc.

**Marylin H. Dahlstrom**
Investor

**Frank E. Diston**
Executive Vice President
Trust Department

**Emanuel A. Floor**
President
Triad Utah

**Robert H. Garff**
President, Ken Garff
Foreign Cars, Inc.

**L. K. Irvine**
Consulting Engineer
Acoustical Engineers, Inc.

**Ellis R. Ivory**
Managing General Partner
Ivory & Co.

**Arch L. Madsen**
President, Bonneville
International Corporation

**Harold W. Milner**
President and Chief
Executive Officer
Americana Hotel &
Realty Corp.

**Newell P. Parkin**
Consultant to the
Chairman

**Aline W. Skaggs**
Director
American Stores Co.

**Dr. Ernest L. Wilkinson**
Physician

**Main Office**
Main at First South

**American Office**
State & 400 South

**Brighton Office**
7220 South Highland Drive

**Carriage Square**
4100 South & Redwood Road

**Copperview Office**
4090 West 3500 South

**Cottonwood Office**
4900 South Highland Drive

**County Office**
888 East 4500 South

**Farmers Office**
530 West 500 South, West Bountiful

**Foothill Office**
1375 Foothill Boulevard

**Holladay Office**
4704 Holladay Boulevard

**Midtown Office**
475 East 200 South

**Midvale Office**
7095 South State

**North Salt Lake Office**
1090 North 500 East

**Operations Center**
440 Lawndale Drive

**Sandy Office**
10625 South State

**Snowbird Office**
Snowbird Ski Resort, Alta

**South Salt Lake Office**
2714 South 300 West

**Sugarhouse Office**
1045 East 2100 South

**Union Square**
9400 South 700 East

**West Jordan Office**
7080 South 1700 West

**West Valley Office**
3620 South 2700 West

**Salt Lake International Airport**
Cashamatic Branch Terminal #1
Cashamatic Branch Terminal #2

Salt Lake City Skyline in 1984

CHAPTER 8

# John Dahlstrom and the Future of Tracy-Collins

While he was not an officer of the bank, John Dahlstrom played an important role in Tracy-Collins affairs after the 1969 purchase. He was president of the holding company, he was on the board of directors, he was one of the executive committee, and he was still the bank's lawyer. Issues such as acquiring American National and Farmers State and preparing and establishing the new Tracy Financial Center demanded his constant attention. He and Gilbert Shelton, during long periods, met daily. Brooke Grant had been a behind-the-scenes partner, by contrast, primarily an investor, but Dahlstrom had a continuous direct role in bank operations during the years of Shelton's chairmanship. It was not an enormous change for him to step in and take over management in 1982.

There were numerous considerations and careful negotiations necessary before an agreement was sealed. But once Shelton decided to leave, the choices were limited. The three partners could have sold their interests; but at the prices potential buyers were willing to pay, Dahlstrom, at least, was unwilling to sell. Grant and Dahlstrom together could have bought out Shelton and continued to operate as partners. But Grant had left direct employment with the bank early on and had developed his own real estate and venture capital business along with other partners. When Shelton withdrew, Grant decided to sell out as well. Dahlstrom then, rather than seeking alternative partners, chose, with his wife Marylin, to assume sole control of the bank. The negotiations that followed were made especially interesting by their intimate familiarity with each other's negotiating styles.[1]

The transaction was completed in March 1982. The Dahlstroms bought the 41 percent interest of Gilbert Shelton for a reported $9 million and Grant's 22 percent for a reported $5 million. The Dahlstroms would own 87 percent of the holding company, the remainder belonging to a few minority shareholders, the Russel Tracy Trust, and the employees' profit-sharing plan. John Dahlstrom took over as chairman of the board and Charles Canfield was promoted to president. Other staff and management remained essentially unchanged.

John Dahlstrom was basically satisfied that the course of the bank he now commanded was correct. He planned no major changes except to "spend more time doing some of the things we do best and less time doing the things that we don't do so well." The things done best included mortgage lending and trust management, both part of Russel Tracy's and James Collins's legacy. Like them, Dahlstrom was betting on the future growth of Utah; he announced at the time of the purchase that "Utah appears to be destined for rapid growth over the next two decades and Tracy-Collins will help in financing that growth."[2]

Tracy's own growth also continued. New branches were added: the South Salt Lake branch in September 1982, the Brighton branch in December 1982, and the Copperview branch in March 1983. And the bank looked at other acquisitions, grabbing headlines in late 1983 in an effort to acquire Continental Bank and Trust. Assets which stood at roughly $45 million in 1969 grew during 1983 to just under $300 million. Under Dahlstrom's tenure, earnings went up 100 percent in 1982 over 1981. In 1983 they leaped another 79 percent.[3]

Banking has changed rapidly in the 1974-84 decade. Legislation designed to deregulate fuzzed many of the boundaries between different financial institutions, allowing nonbank companies to perform many of the services previously restricted to banks. Bankers felt that some of the new rules let others enjoy many of the advantages of banks without meeting the same requirements for safety and soundness. New legislation pending in Congress seeks to address some of these complaints by reasserting some measure of government control.

But wherever banking goes in the future, Tracy-Collins plans to play an important role in Salt Lake's metropolitan area. Dahlstrom foresees more mortgage business with increasing emphasis on rental housing and less on commercial real estate. He also hopes for more emphasis on trust functions. And of course Tracy-Collins will continue to keep pace with the expanding computer revolution. The bank and its holding company have established their own data processing company. Tra-Data, under the able leadership of Phil Trost and Spencer Smith, has taken over the Systematics operation at the service center. One aspect of the business that has been de-emphasized is credit cards. In January 1984 all Tracy-Collins Mastercard accounts were transferred to Crocker

National Bank in California. Dahlstrom explained, "It's a very big business (credit cards) but it has to have high volume to really prosper and we didn't have enough volume." The cards still carry the Tracy-Collins name and electronic recordkeeping makes no acknowledgment of the miles between Utah and California.[4]

Charles Canfield, responding to the question of Tracy-Collins's future, observes:

> I think the issues haven't changed much since during the Depression. One is safety and soundness and two is profitability and three is serving your customers.... I personally would like to see Tracy-Collins maintain the image of safety and soundness and of an institution that people can count on for being a trustee of their deposits and that borrowers can depend on for expertise and being there, helping them through thick and thin if they're good people and honorable people and have the capacity. We want to see them be successful. That makes us successful and that makes the community better. But you need expertise to do it; so I hope that our institution will be always known as one that takes care of its depositors. We take care of our borrowing customers... and utilize the funds that we're trustees of to build and develop the area in a manner that is conducive to the type of society and style of life that we all want and value.[5]

Russel Tracy would not have expressed his sense of responsibility much differently. While aspects of banking have changed, the basic functions and community roles of banks and bankers have not. The banker, like any businessman, seeks profits; his most secure long-term profits come from helping his community grow. John Dahlstrom explained,

> A bank's role is to provide for a flow of funds from the savers to the borrowers. It's a financial intermediary role. That intermediary function is going to have to be carried out by someone if we continue to have a free economy like

> we have. You know in countries where there is no free economy there is no need for money. And if you're in a situation where there is nothing to buy, money becomes worthless. Everything's done on the basis of barter or some other means, so you don't need banks . . . . I stop at a light and I see people going by. Every one of those people is potentially one of my customers. What do they need? Whatever they need is what I want to give them. You're an intermediary; you have a franchise of sorts; and you have to have safety, soundness, reputation, and integrity. But in addition to that, you have to have the willingness to provide the service because that's really all you have to sell—the stopping place, the trade, the service. And the more services, the more innovative and the better-priced, the more successful you'll be.
>
> Traditionally, the banker has been the one that got the Chamber of Commerce going, and the Red Cross and the Boy Scouts. He has good motives in doing that. People are well aware of this. All up and down our organization, we encourage community service. We need to get into community service. That's where our people become acquainted with other people who can open and control accounts. We want to have hundreds of citizens all over town and all over the state and all over the nation that can help us do our job better. We want to be in on the ground floor of anything that's good for this community. That's good for us as well.[6]

One hundred years ago a young Ohioan caught a vision of something lasting in the West. He had come out a few years before with no grandiose expectations. His infirm body had left him stranded in a strange cowtown. But in the West, he found himself able to accept more responsibilities and enjoy more adventures than his sickly childhood had ever allowed him. He found opportunity in a very real sense. Therefore, he decided to be a part of the growing West and to help build it, first in that bustling cowtown of Cheyenne, then in the Mormon metropolis of Salt Lake City. In the process, he set out to leave an institution, a legacy, that would outlive him. Tracy's life was dedicated to these two goals: community service and a business that would endure. We can be certain that Russel Tracy would consider John and Marylin Dahlstrom worthwhile successors. John Dahlstrom's community service—chairmanship of the University of Utah Institutional Council; membership on the boards of the Hotel Utah company, Eyring Research Institute, University of Utah Research Institute, and the Federal Reserve Bank's Salt Lake City branch; and chairmanship of the Salt Lake Area Chamber of Commerce—parallels Tracy's own. The Dahlstroms' dedication to the future of Tracy-Collins Bank and Trust has the strength that comes from protecting what one owns. Tracy-Collins shows every sign of holding on for another hundred years.

# Appendix A

**RUSSEL TRACY'S**
**TEN COMMANDMENTS OF BANKING**

*1*
Not the most but safest loans.

*2*
Once a client always a client.

*3*
Never guarantee a mortgage or the future, but remember

*4*
A moral responsibility is greater than a legal responsibility, and

*5*
A moral obligation should be more binding than a legal obligation.

*6*
Better protect the interest of trusting clients than promote our own.

*7*
Be not ambitious to have the most clients, but rather to have the best protected and satisfied clients in America.

***8***

It is more important to preserve and promote a good name and reputation than to add to our surplus or financial profits.

***9***

We must all leave a record, which others will approve or condemn.

***10***

Conduct the business so no Director will ever be embarrassed.

# Appendix B

**OFFICERS AND DIRECTORS OF TRACY-COLLINS BANK AND TRUST COMPANY AND ITS PREDECESSORS**

Russel L. Tracy, owner and manager of private bank in Cheyenne, Wyoming, 1884-1892

Russel L. Tracy, owner and manager of private bank in Salt Lake City, Utah, 1892-1902

OFFICERS OF RUSSEL L. TRACY COMPANY, 1902-1907
AND OF TRACY LOAN AND TRUST COMPANY, 1908-1944*

*Some of the dates given are approximate.

*Presidents*

Russel L. Tracy, 1902-1933

James W. Collins, 1933-1944

*Vice Presidents*

Luella Tracy, 1902-1907

Newell B. Dayton, 1924-1944

James W. Collins, 1907-1933

*Secretaries*

A. N. McIntosh, 1902-1907

W. P. Hemphill, 1908-1912

George E. Marks, 1912-1919

N. C. Ellis, 1919-1944

*Treasurers*

Russel L. Tracy, 1902-1907

George E. Marks, 1908-1918

W. R. Granville, 1918-1922

Harvey L. Selley, 1922-1932

Newell B. Dayton, 1932-1933

Rufus A. Tracy, Jr., 1933-1945

*Board of Directors*

Russel L. Tracy — 1902-1945
Luella S. Tracy — 1902-1907
A. N. McIntosh — 1902-1908
James W. Collins — 1907-1954
W. P. Hemphill — 1908-1912
Frank B. Stephens — 1912-1940
Leon Sweet — 1919-1958
Joy H. Johnson — 1919-1930
Curtis B. Hawley — 1919-1938
Harvey L. Selley — 1927-1931
Louis Marcus — 1930-1936
N. C. Ellis — 1931-1936
Newell Dayton — 1931-1970
John R. Bruff — 1931-1944
Lee Lovinger — 1936-1952

Scott L. Boyd — 1936-1969
Rufus A. Tracy, Jr. — 1938-1947
Eric W. Ryberg — 1938-1952
Arthur J. Murphy — 1939-1961
Welby S. Emms — 1939-1947
Sid Lockhart — 1939-1952
Paul F. Keyser — 1940-1952
Franklin Riter — 1940-1965
R. Carl Granville — 1940-1967

## OFFICERS AND DIRECTORS OF TRACY-COLLINS TRUST COMPANY, 1944-1960 AND OF TRACY-COLLINS BANK AND TRUST COMPANY, 1960-1984*

### *Chairmen of the Board*

Russel L. Tracy, 1944-1945
James W. Collins, 1954
Newell B. Dayton, 1962-1970
Gilbert W. Shelton, 1970-1982
John A. Dahlstrom, 1982-

### *Vice Chairmen of the Board*

Gilbert Shelton, 1969-1970
Charles Canfield, 1979-

### *Chairmen of the Executive Committee*

Brooke Grant, 1970-1982

### *Presidents*

James W. Collins, 1944-1954
Newell B. Dayton, 1954-1962
Samuel J. Carter, 1962-1969
H. R. Poynter, 1969-1970
Gilbert W. Shelton, 1970-1982
Charles Canfield, 1982-

*Some of the dates given are approximate.

## *Vice Presidents, Senior Vice Presidents, Executive Vice Presidents*

| | |
|---|---|
| Newell B. Dayton | 1944-1954 |
| Rufus A. Tracy, Jr. | 1944-1947 |
| Welby S. Emms | 1944-1947 |
| Samuel J. Carter | 1947-1962 |
| R. Carl Granville | 1948-1957 |
| J. E. Benedict | 1954-1970 |
| H. O. Voget | 1957-1965 |
| J. Lamont Preece | 1957-1969 |
| John T. Clarke | 1958-1959 |
| William H. Von Elm | 1961-1965 |
| Blaine M. Simons | 1965- |
| Ross S. Tyson | 1965-1975 |
| H. Thomas Davis | 1965-1970 |
| Frank E. Diston | 1966- |
| Ben F. Armstrong | 1968- |
| H. Richard Poynter | 1968-1969 |
| Nick D. Lives | 1968-1976 |
| Charles R. Canfield | 1970- |
| R. J. Alleman | 1970- |
| Glen Denkers | 1970- |
| Don Harding | 1970-1971 |
| Laurance C. Peabody | 1970-1971 |
| Leon Lister | 1970-1972 |
| Robert Terry | 1971- |
| Ronald A. Carnago | 1971-1977 |
| John Segerstrom | 1971-1972 |
| Robert Cheney | 1972-1982 |
| John W. Cooper | 1972- |
| L. A. Nielson | 1972-1981 |
| H. J. Gustavson | 1972-1979 |
| William B. Martin | 1972-1983 |

| | |
|---|---|
| Thomas E. Steele | 1972- |
| Ted E. Steers | 1972- |
| Richard A. Wilde | 1972-1974 |
| LeRoy P. Parkin | 1973- |
| Newell P. Parkin | 1973- |
| C. Alan Murdock | 1973-1976 |
| David C. Piggot | 1973-1982 |
| Ronald J. Swenson | 1973-1984 |
| Robert Bagley | 1974-1975 |
| Herbert Gustafson | 1974-1979 |
| Michael R. Giles | 1975-1982 |
| Rex A. Madsen | 1975-1975 |
| Dan Mercer | 1975-1979 |
| Peter K. Ringger | 1975-1983 |
| William Piatt | 1976- |
| William Lapsley | 1976-1982 |
| Edward Sappington | 1976-1978 |
| Louis Burke | 1977-1979 |
| Bart Foulger | 1977- |
| Fred J. Hansen | 1977- |
| Ted May | 1977- |
| Gordon M. Oettli | 1977- |
| Reed D. Newbold | 1977-1979 |
| John C. Slater | 1977-1984 |
| Rex Thornton | 1977-1984 |
| Dale H. Wallberg | 1977-1979 |
| Donald V. Walk | 1977-1979 |
| Robert E. VomDorp | 1978- |
| David Brown | 1978-1981 |
| Vee Carlisle | 1978- |
| Priscilla Hiatt | 1978-1978 |
| Virginia M. Angus | 1979-1980 |
| Douglas L. Hesse | 1979- |
| J. Michael Holt | 1979-1984 |

| | |
|---|---|
| Ben Rietveld | 1980- |
| Marilyn Clark | 1980-1984 |
| Lilian Huetter | 1982- |
| Quinn McKay | 1984- |
| Catherine C. Chanak | 1984- |

*Secretaries*

R. Carl Granville, 1944-1947
Vicki Royer, 1977-1980
Nina Berry, 1983-
Henry E. Ogaard, 1948-1963
J. E. Benedict, 1963-1970
Peter K. Ringger, 1980-1983

*Treasurers*

Rufus A. Tracy, Jr., 1944-1945
Henry E. Ogaard, 1954-1963
J. E. Benedict, 1948-1954

*Cashiers*

William H. Von Elm, 1956-1965
Theodore C. Hauer, 1961
Ross S. Tyson, 1967, 1969
Peter K. Ringger, 1975-1983
Robert P. Jensen, 1965-1967
Fred J. Hansen, 1969-1970
Charles R. Canfield, 1970-1975
Robert E. VomDorp, 1983-

*Directors*

| | |
|---|---|
| W. Prescott Dunn | 1944-1970* |
| Kathryn S. Tracy | 1945-1978 |
| Samuel J. Carter | 1947-1969 |
| Forrest S. Walden | 1952-1968 |
| John Lang | 1952-1960 |
| Frank B. Streator | 1953-1970 |
| Harry E. Carleson | 1954-1965 |

*Some of the dates given are approximate.

| | |
|---|---|
| Sid H. Eliason | 1957-1964 |
| Dilworth S. Woolley | 1961-1979 |
| Gilbert Sheets | 1965-1970 |
| J. E. Benedict | 1967-1970 |
| Frank E. Diston | 1968- |
| H. Richard Poynter | 1968-1970 |
| Gilbert L. Shelton | 1969-1982 |
| John A. Dahlstrom | 1969- |
| Brooke Grant | 1969-1982 |
| Calvin A. Behle | 1969-1982 |
| Charles R. Canfield | 1971- |
| Ronald A. Carnago | 1971-1977 |
| B. F. Armstrong | 1971- |
| Dale R. Curtis | 1972- |
| George C. Furgis | 1972-1974 |
| L. K. Irvine | 1972- |
| William C. Roderick | 1972-1982 |
| Richard A. Wilde | 1972-1974 |
| Newell P. Parkin | 1973- |
| Arch L. Madsen | 1974- |
| James E. Brown | 1977- |
| Peter K. Ringger | 1977-1982 |
| John W. Cooper | 1978-1983 |
| J. Michael Holt | 1979-1984 |
| Ted May | 1979- |
| Richard Christenson | 1982- |
| Marylin Dahlstrom | 1982- |
| Emanuel A. Floor | 1982- |
| Aline Skaggs | 1982- |
| Ronald J. Swenson | 1982-1984 |
| Ernest L. Wilkinson | 1983- |
| Mac Christensen | 1983- |
| Ellis R. Ivory | 1983- |

# Note on the Sources

At the headquarters of Tracy Collins Bank & Trust Company, at 107 South Main Street in Salt Lake City, Utah, are most of the documents and manuscript materials used in preparing this history. These include typescripts and tapes of interviews with bank officials, scrapbooks, circulars, correspondence, minute books, ledgers, and other records. Unless otherwise noted, this is the location of the materials cited and examined. My assistant, John Alley, and I are particularly grateful to Blaine Simons for assistance in making this material available.

Just as Tracy-Collins Bank and Trust's rise in status in the intermountain community was gradual, documentation of the bank's affairs increased over time. We have made considerable use of newspapers during the founding years; they have been valuable for the advertising and business/financial reporting they contain. The company's articles of incorporation were kept by the Secretary of State's office in Salt Lake City and the Utah State Archives holds the *Biennial Reports of the Bank Commissioner.* Present and former staff who granted interviews included Newell Dayton, Blaine Simons, John Dahlstrom, Charles Canfield, and Gilbert Shelton. Stored at the bank are nineteen volumes of scrapbook-style records. These fall into three categories: First, there are four volumes of correspondence labeled Circulars from 1913 to December 31, 1924, Circulars from 1 January 1925 to 1 November 1930, Circulars from 1 January 1931 to

December 1937, and Form Letters, Folders, etc. 1 January 1938 to December 1953. The bulk of these consists of letters sent to client-investors, stockholders, and other important bank customers. Second, there are three volumes labeled Bank Statements: 1916-1923, 1920-1923, and 1931-1932. They contain statements from other banks as well as from Tracy-Collins. Third, there are twelve volumes labeled Scrap Book. These mostly contain advertising, with some newspaper clippings and other material scattered throughout, up until the volume labeled 1949-1956. Halfway through it, all types of records were combined into the one format. There is a marked dropoff in circulars or form letters and a substantial increase in newspaper clippings. This of course reflects an increase in news coverage of Tracy-Collins operations as well as a change in those operations. Wherever possible, for the sake of ease of access to sources by the reader, news clippings from these Scrap Books have been cited to the date of the article rather than to the scrap book volume.

Other archival collections which have been helpful to us include the Western Americana collections at the University of Utah, Utah State University, Brigham Young University, Utah State Historical Society, University of Wyoming, Salt Lake City and County Library, and the private archives of the Historical Department of The Church of Jesus Christ of Latter-day Saints in Salt Lake City.

On general banking history we have often relied on Paul B. Trescott, *Financing American Enterprise: The Story of Commercial Banking* (New York: Harper and Row, 1963). Books and articles on Utah banking history which have been particularly helpful include: Marriner S. Eccles, *Beckoning Frontiers: Public and Personal*

*Recollections*, ed., Sidney Hyman (New York: Alfred A. Knopf, 1951); Leonard J. Arrington, "Banking Enterprises in Utah, 1847-1900," *Business History Review* 29 (December 1955): 312-34; Leonard J. Arrington, *Great Basin Kingdom: An Economic History of the Latter-day Saints, 1830-1900* (Cambridge, Mass.: Harvard University Press, 1958); Roland Stucki, *Commercial Banking in Utah, 1847-1966* (Salt Lake City: Bureau of Economic and Business Research, University of Utah, 1967); Leonard J. Arrington, "Bankers Extraordinary: A History of First Security Corporation, 1928-1973," typescript in possession of the author, Salt Lake City, Utah; Jonathan Bliss, *Merchants and Miners in Utah: The Walker Brothers and Their Bank* (Salt Lake City: Western Epics, 1983).

Several Master's theses, particularly those done under Professor Roland Stucki of the University of Utah, have been very helpful. These include: James M. Lupher, "Development of Utah Banking Legislation, 1847-1963" (MBA thesis, University of Utah, 1964); Howard P. Jones, "The History of Banking in the Utah Economy, 1933-1963" (MBA thesis, University of Utah, 1964); James A. Watson, "A Study of the Growth of Financial Institutions in Utah, 1940-1960" (M.A. thesis, University of Utah, 1961); and C. Dale Randall, "The Historical Development of Branch Banking in the State of Utah" (MBA thesis, University of Utah, 1964).

Other sources are referenced in the notes to each of the chapters, which follow.

# Reference Notes

## *Chapter 1*

1. Aubrey L. Haines, *The Yellowstone Story: A History of Our First National Park* (Yellowstone National Park: Yellowstone Library and Museum Association, 1977), pp. 279-80.
2. Russel Lord Tracy, *Some Experiences of Russel Lord Tracy* (Salt Lake City: privately printed, 1941), p. 34; hereafter cited as Tracy Memoir.
3. Ibid., pp. 39-47, 67-72. Tracy claims this trip was in 1882. Sheridan did make a second visit to Yellowstone that year, but it is apparent from comparing the itinerary and personnel of the two expeditions that Tracy must have been with the 1881 party. See Philip Henry Sheridan, *Report of P. H. Sheridan, dated Sept. 20, 1881, of Expedition through Big Horn Mountains, Yellowstone National Park, etc.* (Washington, D. C.: Government Printing Office, 1882); and Ibid., *Report of an Exploration of Parts of Wyoming, Idaho, and Montana in August and September, 1882* (Washington, D. C.: Government Printing Office, 1882).
4. Unless otherwise indicated, the following account of Tracy's youth comes from Tracy Memoir, pp. 1-32.
5. Carl N. Degler, *At Odds: Women and the Family in America from the Revolution to the Present* (New York: Oxford University Press, 1980), pp. 310-11; Daniel J. Boorstin, *The Americans: The National Experience* (New York: Vintage Books, 1965), pp. 319-20.
6. William H. McNeill, *Plagues and Peoples* (Garden City, New York: Anchor Press/Doubleday, 1976), p. 283.
7. Tracy Memoir, pp. 25-27.
8. Interview with Newell Dayton, Salt Lake City, Utah, 9 November 1983.
9. Cary Abbott, "Cheyenne: The Wild West Sells Its Atmosphere," in Duncan Aikman, ed., *The Taming of the Frontier* (1925;

reprint ed., Freeport, New York: Books for Libraries Press, 1967), pp. 291-319; T. A. Larson, *History of Wyoming* (Lincoln: University of Nebraska Press, 1978), pp. 41-46.

10. I. S. Bartlett, ed., *History of Wyoming* (Chicago: S. J. Clarke Publishing, 1918), p. 558.

11. Larson, *History of Wyoming*, p. 57; *Personal Memoirs of P. H. Sheridan*, 2 vols. (New York, 1888), 2:138; *Annual Report of the Secretary of War* (Washington, D. C., 1882), pp. 270, 274, 293.

12. Bartlett, *History of Wyoming*, pp. 315-18; Jane R. Kendall, "History of Fort Francis E. Warren," *Annals of Wyoming* 18 (January 1946): 2-27; Peggy Dickey Kircus, "Fort David A. Russell: A Study of Its History from 1867 to 1890," *Annals of Wyoming* 40 (October 1968): 161-76; Charles D. Carey, "Camp Carlin," *Annals of Wyoming* 28 (October 1956): 144-50.

13. Carey, "Camp Carlin," p. 147; Larson, *History of Wyoming*, p. 239.

14. Leonard J. Arrington, *The Changing Economic Structure of the Mountain West, 1850-1950*, Utah State University Monograph Series 10, No. 3 (Logan, Utah, 1963), pp. 17, 31, 42, 52.

15. Tracy Memoir, pp. 33-34.

16. Kircus, "Fort David A. Russell," p. 176.

17. Martin F. Schmitt, ed., *General George Crook: His Autobiography* (Norman: University of Oklahoma Press, 1960), pp. 273-74; Tracy Memoir, p. 66.

18. Tracy Memoir, pp. 54-56.

19. Ibid., pp. 73-74.

20. Ibid., pp. 75-76, 89; interview with Newell Dayton.

21. "Circulars from 1913 to Dec. 31, 1924," Tracy-Collins Bank and Trust Scrapbooks, Salt Lake City, Utah; D. M. Frederiksen, "Mortgage Banking in America," *The Journal of Political Economy* 2 (March 1894): 217.

22. Tracy Memoir, pp. 89-90.

23. Larson, *History of Wyoming*, pp. 167-68, 177; W. Turrentine Jackson, "British Interests in the Range Cattle Industry," in Maurice Frink, W. Turrentine Jackson, and Agnes Wright Spring, *When Grass Was King* (Boulder: University of Colorado Press, 1956), pp. 135-330; Walter Prescott Webb, "Windfalls of the Frontier," *Harper's*, November 1951, pp. 74-75.

24. Gene M. Gressley, *Bankers and Cattlemen* (New York: Alfred A. Knopf, 1966), pp. 30-31; *Colorado, New Mexico, Utah, Nevada, Wyoming, and Arizona Gazetteer* (Chicago: R. L. Polk and Co., 1884), p. 544.
25. Lorah B. Chaffin, *Sons of the West: Biographical Account of Early-Day Wyoming* (Caldwell, Idaho: Caxton Printers, 1941), pp. 115-16.
26. Larson, *History of Wyoming*, p. 178.
27. Ibid., pp. 159-62; George W. Rollins, "The Struggle of the Cattleman, Sheepman, and Settler for Control of Lands in Wyoming, 1869-1910" (Ph.D. diss., University of Utah,1951), pp. 294-96; Arrington, "Changing Economic Structure," pp. 31-32, 42-43.
28. Carey, "Camp Carlin," p. 149; Major Lord's house was still standing in 1956 at 22nd and Thames in Cheyenne.
29. John C. Thompson, "In Old Wyoming," *Wyoming State Tribune*, 20 September 1940; C. D. Kirkland, *Photographs of Cheyenne, Wyoming* (New York, 1890).
30. Larson, *History of Wyoming*, pp. 190-94; Reverend Ethelbert Talbot, *My People of the Plains* (New York: Harper and Bros., 1906), pp. 4-5.
31. Larson, *History of Wyoming*, p. 162.
32. Ibid., pp. 158, 195, 296; Gressley, *Bankers and Cattlemen*, pp. 109-10.

## *Chapter 2*

1. Tracy Memoir, p. 90.
2. Ibid., pp. 81, 85.
3. John C. Thompson, "In Old Wyoming," *Wyoming State Tribune*, 20 September 1940, and "Early-Day Local Resident Expires," *Wyoming State Tribune*, 18 May 1945, Clipping Files, Western History Research Center, University of Wyoming, Laramie, Wyoming; Interview with Newell Dayton, Salt Lake City, Utah, 9 November 1983.
4. Dean L. May, "Economic Beginnings," in Richard D. Poll, ed., *Utah's History* (Provo, Utah: Brigham Young University Press, 1978), p. 209.
5. Leonard J. Arrington, *Great Basin Kingdom: An Economic History*

*of the Latter-day Saints, 1830-1900* (Cambridge: Harvard University Press, 1958), p. 199.

6. Leonard J. Arrington and Thomas G. Alexander, *A Dependent Commonwealth: Utah's Economy from Statehood to the Great Depression,* ed. Dean May, Charles Redd Monographs in Western History 4 (Provo, Utah: Brigham Young University Press, 1974), p. 34.
7. Leonard J. Arrington, "The Mormon Tithing House: A Frontier Business Institution," *Business History Review* 28 (March 1954): 24-58; and "Banking Enterprises in Utah, 1847-1880," *Business History Review* 29 (December 1955): 312-34.
8. Arrington, "Banking Enterprises," pp. 315-19; Roland Stucki, *Commercial Banking in Utah, 1847-1966* (Salt Lake City: Bureau of Economic and Business Research, University of Utah, 1967), p. 9.
9. Arrington, "Banking Enterprises," pp. 302-21; Paul B. Trescott, *Financing American Enterprise: The Story of Commercial Banking* (New York: Harper and Row, 1963), p. 47-49.
10. Stucki, *Commercial Banking,* p. 20.
11. Ibid., pp. 20-22.
12. Dean L. May, "Towards a Dependent Commonwealth," in Poll, *Utah's History,* pp. 217-39.
13. Arrington, "Banking Enterprises," p. 334.
14. Stucki, *Commercial Banking,* pp. 77-79; James M. Lupher, "Development of Utah Banking Legislation, 1847-1963" (MBA thesis, University of Utah, 1964), pp. 13-17.
15. John Jay Knox, *A History of Banking in the United States* (New York: Bradford Rhodes, 1903), p. 854; "Business in 1893: Review of the Year by the Bradstreet Agency," *Salt Lake Tribune,* 1 January 1894, p. 12.
16. On this period, see especially Arrington, *Great Basin Kingdom,* pp. 380-412; Leonard J. Arrington and Davis Bitton, *The Mormon Experience: A History of the Latter-day Saints* (New York: Alfred A. Knopf, 1979), pp. 243-61; and Gustive O. Larson, *The "Americanization" of Utah for Statehood* (San Marino, Calif.: Huntington Library & Art Gallery, 1971).
17. "Articles of Incorporation of the Russel L. Tracy Co.," 16 December 1902, Secretary of State's Office, Salt Lake City, Utah.

18. Allan G. Bogue, *Money at Interest: The Farm Mortgage on the Middle Border* (Ithaca, N.Y.: Cornell University Press, 1955), pp. 1-5; W. F. Mappin, "Farm Mortgages and the Small Farmer," *Political Science Quarterly* 4 (September 1889): 435-36.
19. D. M. Frederiksen, "Mortgage Banking in America," *The Journal of Political Economy* 2 (March 1894): 219.
20. Mappin, "Farm Mortgages," p. 435.
21. Bogue, "Money at Interest," pp. 266-67.
22. Ibid., 262-64.
23. J. P. Dunn, Jr., "The Mortgage Evil," *Political Science Quarterly* 5 (March 1890).
24. "Circulars from 1913 to December 31, 1924," Tracy-Collins Bank and Trust Scrapbooks, Salt Lake City, Utah.
25. Arrington, "Banking Enterprises," p. 315, fn. 6.
26. Stucki, *Commercial Banking*, p. 25; Dunn, *"The Mortgage Evil,"* p. 82; *R. L. Polk and Co.'s Salt Lake City Directory, 1891-2 and 1896* (Salt Lake City: R. L. Polk, 1891, 1896).
27. *Salt Lake Tribune*, 11 December 1892, p. 6.
28. Ibid., 28 September 1893, p. 8, and 9 January 1894, p. 8.
29. Ibid., 1 January 1897, p. 7.
30. *Salt Lake Tribune*, 1 January 1892, p. 33.
31. Ibid.; "Extracts from 'Thirty Years' Experience' of the Tracy Loan and Trust Company," in "Circulars from 1913 to December 31, 1924," Tracy-Collins Scrapbooks.
32. "The Business Situation," *Salt Lake Tribune*, 22 December 1892, p. 6.
33. *Salt Lake Tribune*, 28 September 1893, p. 8, and 17 October 1893, p. 8; *Deseret News*, 1 February 1940.
34. "Extracts from 'Thirty Years' Experience'."
35. "The Real Estate Situation," *Salt Lake Tribune*, 6 May 1894, p. 5.
36. Bogue, "Money at Interest," p. 267; *Salt Lake Tribune*, 11 January 1894, p. 8, and 1 February 1894, p. 8.
37. Raymond Elmer Higgins, "The Architectural History of the Salt Lake City and County Building" (M. A. thesis, University of Utah, 1978), pp. 56-67; Burtch W. Beall, Jr., and Peter L. Goss,

"Utah's Architectural Heritage: City and County Building, Salt Lake City," *Utah Architect* 54 (Autumn 1973): 20-24.

38. Dayton Interview, 9 November 1983.

39. *Salt Lake Tribune*, 1 January 1895, p. 22.

40. *Salt Lake City Directories*, 1894-1916; *Salt Lake Tribune*, various issues, 1894-1916; "Trust Company in New Home, Palatial Quarters Are Ready," *Salt Lake Telegram*, 28 August 1916.

41. Cf. Bogue, "Money of Interest," pp. 125-26; Lupher, "Utah Banking Legislation," p. 36.

42. "Articles of Incorporation of the Russel L. Tracy, Co.," MS. Secretary of State's Office, Salt Lake City, Utah.

## *Chapter 3*

1. "Ten Commandments to the Officers of Tracy Loan and Trust Co.," Tracy Memoir, p. 103.

2. Interview with Newell Dayton, Salt Lake City, Utah, 9 November 1983.

3. Leonard J. Arrington, "The Commercialization of Utah's Economy: Trends and Developments from Statehood to 1910," in Arrington and Alexander, *A Dependent Commonwealth*, pp. 3-34.

4. Ibid., pp. 11-12; Roland Stucki, *Commercial Banking in Utah, 1847-1966* (Salt Lake City: Bureau of Economic and Business Research, University of Utah, 1967), pp. 25-26.

5. *Salt Lake Tribune*, 1 January 1906, p. 16; 1 January 1908, pp. 1-2; 2 February 1910, p. 34; Thomas G. Alexander, "The Burgeoning of Utah's Economy: 1910-1918," in Leonard J. Arrington and Thomas G. Alexander, *A Dependent Commonwealth: Utah's Economy from Statehood to the Great Depression*, ed., Dean May, Charles Redd Monographs in Western History, 4 (Provo, Utah: Brigham Young University Press, 1974), p. 34.

6. "Circulars from 1913 to December 31, 1924," Tracy Collins Bank and Trust Scrapbooks, Salt Lake City, Utah.

7. *Salt Lake Tribune*, 2 November 1907; "Circulars from 1913 to December 31, 1924."

8. Gilbert C. Fite and Jim E. Reese, *An Economic History of the United States* (Boston: Houghton Mifflin, 1973), p. 443: "Circulars from 1913 to December 31, 1924."

9. "Circulars from 1913 to December 31, 1924."
10. "First Mortgage Loans Offered January, 1915, by the Tracy Loan and Trust Company," and "First Mortgage Loans Offered October, 1915, by the Tracy Loan and Trust Company," Tracy-Collins Scrapbooks.
11. "Articles of Incorporation of the Russel L. Tracy, Co.," 16 December 1902 and 21 February 1908; Interview, 9 November 1983.
12. "Certificate of Amendment to the Articles of Incorporation of the Tracy Loan & Trust Company, 30 November 1914.
13. Lupher, "Development of Utah Banking Legislation: 1847-1963" (MBA thesis, University of Utah, 1964), pp. 22, 35.
14. State of Utah, *Report of the Bank Commissioner, 1913-1914* (Salt Lake City: Arrow Press, 1915), p. 105.
15. Tracy Loan and Trust Company, *The Future of Your Affairs* (Salt Lake City, 1915).
16. Ralph Parlette, *Making Good with Mildred,* n.d.
17. "Articles of Incorporation," 21 February 1908.
18. "Circulars from 1913 to December 31, 1924."
19. Virginia Rishel, *Wheels to Adventure: Bill Rishel's Western Routes* (Salt Lake City: Howe Brothers, 1983), pp. 49, 55; "Circulars from 1913 to December 31, 1924"; "Advertising, 1915 to 1917," Tracy-Collins Scrapbooks.
20. State of Utah, *Report of the Bank Commissioner, 1915-1916* (Salt Lake City: Arrow Press, 1916), p. 106; and *Report of the Bank Commissioner, 1921-1922* (Salt Lake City: Arrow Press, 1922), pp. 111-15.
21. "Circulars from 1913 to December 31, 1924"; *Salt Lake Telegram,* 29 July 1924, in "Scrapbook, 1917-1925," Tracy-Collins Scrapbooks.
22. "Extracts from 'Thirty Years' Experience' of the Tracy Loan and Trust Company," in "Circulars from 1913 to December 31, 1924."
23. "Minutes of Special Meeting of the Stockholders of Tracy Loan and Trust Company," 26 March 1912, in "Articles of Incorporation of the Russel L. Tracy Co."
24. "Circulars from 1913 to December 31, 1924."

25 "Bank Statements, 1931-1932," Tracy-Collins Scrapbooks.

26. "Circulars from 1913 to December 31, 1924"; *Salt Lake Telegram*, 28 August 1916; *Deseret News*, 28 August 1916; *Salt Lake Herald-Republican*, 27 August 1916; *Salt Lake Tribune*, 27 August 1916.

27. On the completed building, see the sources cited above, plus John S. McCormick, *The Historic Buildings of Downtown Salt Lake City* (Salt Lake City: Utah State Historical Society, 1983), pp. 71-72.

28. "Circulars from 1913 to December 31, 1924."

29. *Salt Lake Herald-Republican*, January 1920, in "Circulars from 1913 to December 31, 1924."

30. "Circulars from 1913 to December 31, 1924"; and "Advertising 1915 to 1917."

31. Leonard J. Arrington, "Bankers Extraordinary: A History of First Security Corporation, 1928-1973," typescript in possession of the author, Salt Lake City, Utah, pp. 258-61.

32. Stucki, *Commercial Banking of Utah*, pp. 35-36; "Circulars from 1913 to December 31, 1924."

33. Alexander, "The Burgeoning of Utah's Economy."

34. Thomas G. Alexander, "The Economic Consequences of the War: Utah and the Depression of the Early 1920s," in Arrington and Alexander, *A Dependent Commonwealth*, p. 83; Stucki, *Commercial Banking in Utah*, pp. 39-47.

35. "Bank Statements, 1931-1932."

36. "Circulars from 1913 to December 31, 1924," and "Bank Statements, 1931-1932."

## Chapter 4

1. Interview with Blaine Simons, Salt Lake City, Utah, 10 January 1984, typescript and tapes in the possession of Tracy-Collins Bank and Trust Company, Salt Lake City, Utah.

2. Tracy Loan and Trust Company, *A Review of Forty-Three Years' Experience, 1884-1927* (Salt Lake City, 1927); and *Methods and Results: A Review of Forty-Seven Years' Experience, 1884-1931* (Salt Lake City, 1931); *Salt Lake Telegram*, 2 January, 25 December 1928; *Salt Lake Tribune*, 24 December 1929, 1 January 1931.

3. Tracy Memoir, pp. 125-27, 159; Simons interview, 10 January 1984.

4. Simons interview, 10 January 1984.

5. Interview with Newell Dayton, 9 November 1983.

6. Sources disagree about when the meeting with Ralph Nielson and the tradition of Thanksgiving dinners for newboys began, but 1902 seems the most likely date for the former and 1903 for the latter. Micky's ditty is from *Salt Lake Telegram*, 29 November 1917. On Tracy's aid to the newsboys see Thanksgiving week issues of the *Salt Lake Telegram*, *Salt Lake Tribune*, or *Salt Lake Herald-Republican* between 1912 and 1940; and Tracy Memoir, pp. 131-55.

7. Herbert B. Maw, *Adventures with Life* (Salt Lake City, privately published, 1978), p. 22. Excerpts from the inauguration address are in the Salt Lake *Telegram* for 6 January 1941.

8. Tracy Memoir, pp. 157, 161-65; *Salt Lake Tribune*, 19 September 1936; Miriam B. Murphy, "'Of Benefit and Interest to the Children of Salt Lake City'—the Tracy Aviary," *Utah Historical Quarterly* 48 (Summer 1980): 261-70.

9. Tracy Memoir, pp. 107-9; Kate B. Carter, ed., *Our Pioneer Heritage*, 20 vols. (Salt Lake City: Daughters of Utah Pioneers, 1958-1977), 10: 339-41.

10. *Deseret News*, 14 August 1954; *Salt Lake Tribune*, 15 and 16 August 1954; "From Errand Boy to President," in "Circulars, 1/1931-12/1937," Tracy-Collins Scrapbooks; Simons interview, 10 January 1984.

11. "Circulars from 1/1/25 to Nov. 1, 1930," Tracy-Collins Scrapbooks; State of Utah, *Report of the Bank Commissioner, 1921-1922* (Salt Lake City,1930), p. 20.

12. "Circulars from 1/1/25 to Nov. 1, 1930"; *Methods and Results*; Tracy Loan and Trust Company, *Why Make a Will? Advantage of a Trust Company, Laws of Descent* (Salt Lake City, 1928).

13. "Circulars from 1/1/25 to Nov. 1, 1930"; Simons interview, 10 January 1984.

14. *Methods and Results; Coast Banker*, 20 February 1931.

15. "Circulars from 1/1/25 to Nov. 1, 1930."

16. Gilbert C. Fite and Jim E. Reese, *An Economic History of the United States* (Boston: Houghton Mifflin, 1973), pp. 504-6.

17. Thurman Arnold, "The Crash—and What It Meant," in Isabel Leighton, ed., *The Aspirin Age, 1919-1941* (New York: Simon and Schuster, 1949), p. 222.
18. Marriner S. Eccles, *Beckoning Frontiers: Public and Personal Recollections*, ed. Sidney Hyman (New York: Alfred A. Knopf, 1951), pp. 54-55.
19. Roland Stucki, *Commercial Banking in Utah, 1847-1966* (Salt Lake City: Bureau of Economic and Business Research, University of Utah, 1967), pp. 41, 43.
20. Trescott, *Financing American Enterprise*, pp. 202-5.
21. Simons interview, 10 January 1984; "Circulars, 1/193112/1937"; "Bank Statements, 1931-1932," Tracy-Collins Scrapbooks.
22. "Circulars, 11/1931-12/1937."
23. Arrington, "Bankers Extraordinary: A History of First Security Corporation, 1928-1973," pp. 136-41, typescript in the possession of the author, Salt Lake City, Utah; Eccles, *Beckoning Frontiers*, pp. 63-69.
24. "Circulars, 1/1/1931-12/1937."
25. Simons interview, 10 January 1984.
26. "Circulars, 1/1/1931-12/1937."
27. Simons interview, 10 January 1984.
28. Paul B. Trescott, *Financing American Enterprise, The Story of Commercial Banking* (New York: Harper and Row, 1963), pp. 207-8; Arrington, "Bankers Extraordinary," pp. 165-67.
29. "Circulars, 1/1/1931-12/1937"; "Bank Statements, 1931-1932."
30. Ibid.

## *Chapter 5*

1. "Circulars, 1/1931-12/1937," Tracy-Collins Scrapbooks.
2. Ibid., and "Form Letters, Folders, etc., 1/1/38-12/53," Tracy-Collins Scrapbooks.
3. Ibid.
4. Marriner S. Eccles, *Beckoning Frontiers: Public and Personal Recollections*, ed., Sidney Hyman (New York: Alfred A. Knopf, 1951), pp. 144, 149.
5. Ibid., pp. 150-52; Leonard J. Arrington, "Bankers Extraordinary:

A History of First Security Corporation, 1928-1973," pp. 166-67, typescript in possession of the author, Salt Lake City; "Housing," *The Index* 26 (Spring 1946): 2.

6. "Housing," p. 3; Arrington, "Bankers Extraordinary," pp. 149-50.
7. "Housing," p. 3; Arrington, "Bankers Extraordinary," p. 167; Eccles, *Beckoning Frontiers*, pp. 299-303.
8. Paul B. Trescott, *Financing American Enterprise: The Story of Commercial Banking* (New York: Harper and Row, 1963), pp. 186, 209.
9. *Salt Lake Telegram*, 3 June 1938.
10. "Form Letters, Folders, etc., 1/1/38-12/53."
11. *Salt Lake Tribune*, 19 December 1938; *Deseret News*, 1 February 1940.
12. Gilbert C. Fite and Jim E. Reese, *An Economic History of the United States* (Boston: Houghton Mifflin, 1973), pp. 543-45; Eccles, *Beckoning Frontiers*, pp. 344-46.
13. Eccles, *Beckoning Frontiers*, pp. 344-46; Trescott, *Financing American Enterprise*, pp. 213-15; Arrington, "Bankers Extraordinary," pp. 172-74.
14. "Form Letters, Folders, etc., 1/1/38-12/53"; Interview with Blaine Simons, 10 January 1984.
15. "Form Letters, Folders, etc., 1/1/38-12/53."
16. Ibid., "Scrap Book, 1941-1949," Tracy-Collins Scrapbooks.
17. "Form Letters, Folders, etc., 1/1/38-12/53"; "Tracy Loan & Trust Company Certificate Amending Name to Tracy-Collins Trust Company," 6 May 1944, Secretary of State's Office, Salt Lake City, Utah.
18. Simons interview, 10 January 1984; *Deseret News*, 6 May 1944; *Salt Lake Tribune*. 26 April 1953.
19. *Salt Lake Tribune*, 18 and 19 May 1945; *Deseret News*, 18 May 1945; *Salt Lake Tribune*, 26 April 1953.
20. Leonard J. Arrington, *The Changing Economic Structure of the Mountain West: 1850-1950*, Utah State University Monograph Series 10, no. 3 (Logan, Utah, 1963), pp. 24-25; Leonard J. Arrington and George Jensen, *The Defense Industry of Utah*, Utah State Planning Program (Logan: Utah State University,

1965); John E. Christensen, "The Impact of World War II," in Poll, *Utah's History,* pp. 497-507.

21. Roland Stucki, *Commercial Banking in Utah: 1847-1966* (Salt Lake City: Bureau of Economic and Business Research, University of Utah, 1967), pp. 69-71.
22. Trescott, *Financing American Enterprise,* p. 229.
23. "Housing," p. 1; Fite and Reese, *An Economic History of the United States,* p. 598.
24. *Salt Lake Tribune,* 25 January 1945.
25. "Form Letter, Folders, etc., 1/1/38-12/53"; Scrap Book, 1941-1949"; *Deseret News,* 18 July 1955.
26. State of Utah, *Biennial Reports of the Bank Commissioner* (Salt Lake City, 1942, 1944, 1948, 1950, 1952).
27. "Form Letters, Folders, etc., 1/1/38-12-53."
28. *Salt Lake Tribune,* 25 November 1950, 27 May 1951, 4 January 1953; *Deseret News,* 4 January 1953.
29. *Salt Lake Tribune,* 26 April 1953.
30. *Electrical West* 3 (September 1953): 6.

## Chapter 6

1. Roland Stucki, *Commercial Banking in Utah: 1847-1966* (Salt Lake City: Bureau of Economic and Business Research, University of Utah, 1967), p. 69; State of Utah, *Biennial Reports of the Bank Commissioner,* 1944-1954.
2. Howard P. Jones, "The History of Banking in the Utah Economy, 1933-1963" (M. B. A. thesis, University of Utah, 1964), pp. 60-61.
3. State of Utah, *Biennial Reports of the Bank Commissioner,* 1944-1954; Interview with Blaine Simons, 10 January 1984.
4. *Salt Lake Tribune,* 17 January 1954.
5. Interview with Newell Dayton, 9 November 1983.
6. Ibid.
7. Dan Valentine, "Nothing Serious," *Salt Lake Tribune,* 15 May 1954; "Scrap Book, 1949-1956," Tracy-Collins Scrapbooks.
8. *Deseret News,* 16 August 1954; also see *Deseret News,* 14 August 1954; *Salt Lake Tribune,* 15, 16 August 1954.

9. *Salt Lake Tribune*, 23 October 1953.
10. Ibid., 8 April 1956.
11. *Provo Daily Herald*, 17 May 1955; "Scrap Book, 1949-1966."
12. "Scrap Book, 1949-1956," "Amendments to the Articles of Incorporation of Tracy-Collins Trust Company," 1 March 1956, Secretary of State's Office, Salt Lake City, Utah; Simons interview, 10 January 1984; *American Banker*, September 1965.
13. Utah Bank Commission, *Laws of the State of Utah... As Amended January, 1964* (Salt Lake City: State of Utah, 1964), p. 23; Stucki, *Commercial Banking in Utah*, p. 71.
14. "Amendments to the Articles of Incorporation of Tracy-Collins Trust Company," 1 March 1956; *Salt Lake Tribune*, 28 February 1956.
15. James A. Watson, "A Study of the Growth of Financial Institutions in Utah, 1940-1960" (M. A. thesis, University of Utah, 1961), pp. 73, 84.
16. Ibid., *Salt Lake Tribune*, 22 June 1960; *Deseret News*, 22 June 1960.
17. C. Dale Randall, "The Historical Development of Branch Banking in the State of Utah" (M. B. A. thesis, University of Utah, 1964), pp. 3, 9, 33-34.
18. Ibid., p. 34.
19. Ibid., pp. 12, 42; Stucki, *Commercial Banking in Utah*, pp. 57-58, 62-63.
20. Jones, "The History of Banking in the Utah Economy," pp. 16-17.
21. Randall, "Historical Development of Branch Banking," pp. 41-42.
22. *Holladay Neighbor*, 27 June 1956; Jones, "History of Banking in the Utah Economy," p. 18; "Scrap Book, 1956-1962," Tracy-Collins Scrapbooks.
23. State of Utah, *Biennial Report of the Bank Commissioner*, 1958; *Holladay Neighbor*, 30 January 1957.
24. *Western Banker*, September 1963; *Salt Lake Tribune*, 2 June 1963.
25. *Salt Lake Tribune*, 3, 10 December 1961.

26. *Holladay Neighbor*, 19 March 1964; *Salt Lake Tribune*, 6 March 1964, 24 August, 9 September 1967.
27. *Salt Lake Tribune*, 23 October 1963.
28. *Intermountain Contractor*, 27 August 1965; *Salt Lake Tribune*, 20 July 1965; *Western Banker*, October 1965.
29. State of Utah, *Bicentennial Reports of the Bank Commissioner*, 1956-1966.
30. *Salt Lake Tribune*, 7, 8, 10 January 1967.
31. "Scrap Book, 1956-1962"; "Scrap Book, 1963-1966," Tracy-Collins Scrapbooks.
32. Ibid.
33. Ibid.
34. Dayton interview, 9 November 1983.

### Chapter 7

1. *Western Banker*, August 1968; *Deseret News*, 27 June 1969.
2. *Salt Lake Tribune*, 14 January and 9 February 1969.
3. The discussion of the 1969 sale of Tracy-Collins Bank and Trust is based primarily on interviews with Newell Dayton, 9 November 1983; John Dahlstrom, 1 March 1984; and Gilbert Shelton, 28 March 1984; as well as on contemporary newspaper accounts.
4. *Salt Lake Tribune*, 9 December 1969.
5. Dahlstrom interview, 1 March 1984; *Salt Lake Tribune*, 3 December 1969.
6. Shelton interview, 28 March 1984; *Salt Lake Tribune*, 5 April 1970.
7. Shelton interview, 28 March 1984.
8. "Scrapbooks, 1970-1971, 1971-1974, 1974-1979," Tracy-Collins Scrapbooks.
9. Robert S. Olpin, "Contemporary Utah Artists Exhibition," *Utah Holiday* 3 (September 1979); Scrapbook, 1974-1979.
10. *Salt Lake Tribune*, 30 December 1970; "Triumphant Break from the Traditional," *Intermountain Contractor*, 24 December 1971.
11. *Salt Lake Tribune*, 30 July 1976 and June 1981; Dahlstrom interview, 1 March 1984; Shelton interview, 28 March 1984.

12. *Salt Lake Tribune,* 11 March 1971; Scrapbook, 1971-1974.
13. Shelton interview, 28 March 1984.
14. *Salt Lake Tribune,* 31 January 1974 and 3 July 1975.
15. Dahlstrom interview, 1 March 1984; Shelton interview, 28 March 1984; *Salt Lake Tribune,* 1 December 1971.
16. *Deseret News,* 29 September 1979.
17. *Salt Lake Tribune,* 29 September 1979.
18. Interview with Charles Canfield, 1 March 1984; *Salt Lake Tribune,* 1 December 1936, 10 February 1973, 9 May 1973, 4 September 1974; *Deseret News,* 3 May 1973, 25 March 1974; *Mountain States Banker* (August 1974).
19. Shelton interview, 28 March 1984; Canfield interview, 1 March 1984; Dahlstrom interview, 1 March 1984.
20. Ibid.
21. The following employees have served more than twenty years with Tracy-Collins: Blaine Simons (50); Lou Burke (32); Maxine Kreipl (29); Ralph Webb (28); Iola Petersen (28); Virginia Angus (26); Nelda Behunin (24); Shirley Rich (23); Inge Goudriaan (23); Robert Alleman (23); Maurine Page (23); Fred Hansen (22); Catherine Chanak (22); Betty Smith (20).
22. Tracy-Collins Scrapbooks.

## *Chapter 8*

1. Interview with John Dahlstrom, 1 March 1984; interview with Gilbert Shelton, 28 March 1984.
2. *Deseret News,* 2-3 April 1982.
3. *Deseret News,* 29 January 1984.
4. Interview with Charles Canfield, 1 March 1984; Dahlstrom interview, 1 March 1984; *Deseret News,* 29 January 1984.
5. Canfield interview, 1 March 1984.
6. Dahlstrom interview, 1 March 1984.

# Index